KERRY KIRWAN
BLOOM & BURN

11:11

A TRANSFORMATIONAL JOURNEY OF AWAKENING

Kerry Kirwan/IngramSpark

Melbourne, VICTORIA

Copyright © 2019 by **Kerry Kirwan**

All rights reserved. No part of this publication may be reproduced, distributed or transmitted in any form or by any means, without prior written permission.

Kerry Kirwan/IngramSpark
www.kerrykirwan.com

Bloom & Burn: A Transformational Journey of Awakening/Kerry Kirwan. 1st ed.

ISBN 978-0-6484846-0-1

Text editing and book design by Dr Juliette Lachemeier @ The Erudite Pen
www.theeruditepen.com

Cover design by Christian Hildebrand

This book is my gift to Patricia Chong.
Patricia serves the divine uncompromisingly.

In the presence of a spiritual master, you can realise your own divinity.

My book is an expression of
the price that was paid
to realise God.

May all beings be happy, may all beings be peaceful, may all beings be blissful.

Acknowledgements

Thank you to all who have shared my life's journey.
I love you all unconditionally.

Dear readers, thank you for choosing to read my book,
Bloom & Burn
11:11
A Transformational Journey of Awakening.

Everything except love is devoured by love.

–Rumi

contents

Foreword 1
Introduction 3
Answering the Call to Awaken 7
Life Before the Call to Awaken 13
Opening to the Unknown 25
Time for Change and Growth 31
My Teacher, My Master, My Greatest Reflection 39
The Work 49
The Wounded Feminine 73
Myanmar and the Twin Flame Journey 85
Beyond Religion: Christ Consciousness and the Second Coming of Christ 103
A Forgotten Language: Symbolism, Intuition and Dreams 111
11:11 Its Purpose and Meaning 123
Important Realisations 129
Conclusion 141

Foreword

Bloom & Burn is a story of divine grace in action; it is a personal biography about a seeker on a spiritual quest. Kerry was determined to know the answer to two very important questions: Who am I and why am I here?

Kerry reveals how her journey unfolded once she heard the call and accepted her invitation to awaken. This book is her personal story of suffering, longing, devotion and realisation. She shares her experiences and the many synchronicities that unfolded within these experiences.

The title *Bloom & Burn* is an analogy that best describes her journey of awakening as both aspects transpired simultaneously. The story of her journey in its totality is non-linear and all-encompassing. *Bloom & Burn* symbolises the entirety of her experience, although it has been encapsulated within a story that contains what appear to be numerous separate experiences.

Donna Dolan

Introduction

If you are about to read *Bloom & Burn*, it means that you have heard your call to awaken. Will you answer it?

I believe that at this point in time there is an opportunity for humanity to make a great transition within. In times past, only a select few were called and invited to make this transition. Humanity is on the brink of monumental change, and now it is time for many to embark upon a personal journey of discovery and spiritual awakening.

How do we answer the call to awaken? What is required? An invitation will be sent out to the masses; many have been prepared and are unconsciously waiting for it to arrive. The 11:11 sequence is a code within our DNA signifying that it is time to remember who we are. Now is the time to move beyond dualities and resolve our inner conflicts so we can balance our masculine and feminine polarities. We all have an inner masculine and feminine, but the masculine has dominated and the feminine has been repressed. An inner union awaits – a divine marriage will occur within once these forces are balanced. This process will allow our heart centres to open so the

love that we are can be experienced. This is what is known as Christ consciousness. And our invitation to awaken to this consciousness will arrive in a way that is unique and significant to us and our personal journey thus far.

What does it mean to awaken? What is the transition? How do we begin to understand what we know but have long forgotten? *Bloom & Burn* will guide those who have chosen to remember and accept the invitation. My book is written and explained in a way that is understandable, simple and direct. We can achieve an awakened state of being exactly where we find ourselves. The divine will not discriminate against those who accept this invitation, nor will it require that we be uprooted from our current circumstances, our family or our professions. The purpose of this book is to simplify all that I have discovered about awakening and to share aspects of my personal journey, along with the wisdom that I gained from my experiences.

We can awaken to our greatness – the divine essence within. What if I told you that we have already bloomed and we have always been what we are awakening to? It is just that we have forgotten who we are and won't believe this statement until we have experienced it for ourselves. Most of humanity has fallen asleep and lives life unconsciously.

The truth has been buried, but where is it buried? It is deep within us; it has always existed and is waiting to be acknowledged. And life will continually invite us to discover and experience the truth for ourselves. All that keeps us small and limited is what we have identified with personally and collectively, and this creates a separate, individual ego self. Our ego self contains the accumulation of all our personalised experiences that have become layered upon our being.

What veils the divine has two components – the first being personal identification. This is all that we have become identified with throughout our current lives, all that we have been conditioned by and attached to: our titles, status, beliefs, patterns, possessions, painful experiences and any unresolved emotions. All of these create an ego self and an inner imbalance between our masculine and feminine aspects. We are not our experiences, we are not what we feel, we are not what we do, nor are we what we have unconsciously accumulated.

The second component veiling the divine is our collective identification. This is represented by the same components and is the accumulation of all that is unresolved from the past, via previous generations, and which is unconsciously passed on to the next generation. All of these aspects must be recognised and surrendered for our consciousness to expand beyond self-imposed limitations

Imagine we are all dormant seeds that have been germinating, kept in the dark, and when the circumstances are perfect, there will be some movement and the seed will split open. We may start to feel restless; perhaps, we will acknowledge that we are unhappy. We may feel lost or disconnected, or have a sense of emptiness and or depression. We may have had a major event in our lives – a divorce, an accident or the death of a loved one. It may just be that we feel that we don't belong, or it could be that we have never felt like we have belonged. For all of our lives, we may have been ignoring what we no longer can.

Life is our fertiliser. At this point, our choice to remain dormant will be eliminated, particularly if we are the seed that has been chosen to grow. The appropriate conditions, and our driving force to reach the light, will be orchestrated from the story we are creating and have lived. This will generate the growth and the understanding for us to bloom. Life and what we experience will become more intense. A fire will ignite that destroys all illusion so what we have forgotten will begin to make its presence felt.

Kerry Kirwan

1

Answering the Call to Awaken

In 1989, I was twenty-four years old and happily married with a one-year-old child. We lived in a modest home and were financially secure, complete with all the trappings of a successful modern-day life. We were also thinking of adding to our family by having a second child.

Life was great, but almost overnight, everything changed for me. It was like a switch was flicked within and something unknown started to stir. I suddenly felt discontent, restless and uncomfortable with myself and my life.

Out of nowhere, I started to question what life was all about: Who am I? Why am I here? These questions began to stir something deep within my soul. I had practically achieved all that I had ever dreamed of having and what I thought life was about, yet I unexpectedly felt so unfulfilled.

This inner restlessness was my personal call to awaken, not that I knew it back then. All I knew was that I desperately wanted to know the answers to those existential life questions arising within me. The pull and intensity those questions evoked were so great and unknowingly so important. I now

recognise that my call to awaken could never have been refused because the driving force behind those questions was so intense.

Within a week or so of my existential questioning, I had a strong, random inner urge to read a book. I had never willingly read a book, especially one that had more than ten pages! I did not find reading captivating or interesting at all, but for some unknown reason I had a desire to visit the local library and get myself a book to read. Upon arrival, I felt totally overwhelmed. I had no idea what type of book I was even looking for. I instinctively knew that I wasn't going to choose a fictional book; I wanted something real. My bewilderment must have shown on my face as the next thing I knew after explaining my dilemma to the librarian, she was directing me to the autobiography section.

To my delight, about eight titles in, I was immediately attracted to one book in particular. I took it off the shelf, scanned its pages and read the back cover. Oh my God, I had found it! I had actually found the book I knew was meant for me. Delighted and excited, I took it to the counter. It was entitled *Out on a Limb* by Shirley MacLaine.

The buried seed within me had definitely split open and movement had begun. I couldn't wait to begin reading. I was totally blown away and truly fascinated by the content of the book. I wondered why I had never been introduced to any of this spiritual information before now; it was like I'd been dying of thirst all my life and someone had only just given me a drink of water.

I devoured *Out on a Limb* and was utterly enthralled reading a chapter that described Shirley's experience in Peru whereby she witnessed the channelling of an entity through the body of another. I was utterly intrigued by this and thought to myself, *Wow! What an experience that would be!* I had never heard of such a thing. Ever! I continued reading like a thirsty camel, absorbing all that I could to counteract the drought and dehydration that my spirit had suffered up until that point.

Approximately a week after finding Shirley's book, a former family friend, who I had not seen or heard from in a long time (twenty years to be exact) made contact to reconnect. The floating thoughts that were in my mind after so many years without contact were, *Why did he choose to reconnect now? It was so random and unexpected.*

As fate would have it, this family friend's daughter actually channelled a spiritual entity! When I heard this, the hair on the back of my neck stood on end, and my skin bristled with goose bumps. After all, I had only just read in my newly discovered book *Out on a Limb* about this strange occurrence.

I knew I had to experience what this friend's daughter had to offer. Prior to meeting her, I experienced a mixture of excitement, exhilaration, fear and trepidation all rolled into one. Upon meeting her, my being was totally electrified and excited for what I was about to experience. I could hardly believe how it had all come about and the amazing synchronicity of it all.

Throughout the evening session, we all had the opportunity to ask the channelled entity questions on many topics. I generally sat back and listened intently. I never really felt the urge to ask any questions, unlike others. I was probably a little too shy, and it was not my nature to draw attention to myself. The channelled entity was called Ashram; I perceived Ashram as a he, as did many others, and he assumed a very peaceful and calm presence. The atmosphere created by his presence was incredibly loving and all-encompassing, and I was so grateful to

bask in it. I became a regular at the weekly spirit-channelled gatherings. I enjoyed my time there immensely as it was an opportunity to connect with many like-minded individuals.

During this time, my spiritual thirst grew to the point of feeling like I was a 'spiritual alcoholic' who could hardly wait for the next session. Attending the channelled sessions was the highlight of my week, and it was a stepping-stone on a journey that had seemed to have only just begun.

However, I now accept that my journey to awakening began even before the moment I was born, and the destination was always with me. The 1989 portion of my journey was a point where it became more intensified, and the destination was as close and yet as far as it would ever be.

My unconsciousness and the layers that veiled the destination that was always present within took many years to uncover. Years of dedication, desire, devotion and an uncontrollable longing powered the process of seeking the truth behind those two big questions: Who am I and why am I here?

Returning to 1989, I had many strange happenings over the coming months. I would describe my personality as introverted, although I was very determined and strong-willed. I was a Virgo perfectionist and often a very impatient person, and these traits both helped and hindered my deep desire to know and experience what I was seeking. I believe my impatience caused a lot unnecessary problems and experiences along the way, but it was my determination that helped me through them.

I started to read other spiritual-related books but still I felt no more understanding in relationship to my questions, especially as to who I was. As I was reading, I was continually drawn to the word 'divine'. It kept appearing in all the texts, and it was the main word that caught my attention. It stood out almost like it was glowing and dancing on the page, as if it were showing me that this was the answer to my question. I felt the word re-playing over and over in my head.

I unconsciously questioned from within because at this stage, I hadn't consciously understood that I had an ability to connect with my higher self and was actually doing it in that moment – and had done so most of my life without realising it. I asked, 'Is this what you're telling me I am? I'm divine?' This made no sense to me. What did divine even mean? I had no clue, except that at the time there was an '80s overweight transvestite singer who called himself Divine – an eccentric male dressed as a female in the most unflattering way. This was not the answer I had hoped for.

The changes that were taking place within me caused a lot of disruption in my immediate relationships, particularly in the beginning. Change was happening rapidly, and it was at times frightening but at the same time exciting and new. I learned to work through everything that surfaced within my relationships over the years that followed. I saw the disruptions, reflections and projections as opportunities to grow and understand myself and others beyond them. Many years later, a lot of the pieces of the puzzle of my journey eventually found their place. Once they did, I was able to see more clearly, like an eagle that has greater view and perspective once it has risen high enough.

Prior to all this existential probing, I was just like a star in the night sky minding my own business and living my life, twinkling and sparkling without any thought of why. After I'd questioned the meaning of my existence, it was like I was ignited. The intensity within me grew and grew, and it couldn't be

stopped. The pull and the driving force were beyond my control and were unrelenting. My being suddenly felt like a shooting star, burning up, disintegrating and hurtling through the universe at a speed beyond belief.

I had no idea what the end result might be; I had no choice other than to just allow what was happening to happen. It was an unimaginable intensity that continued for many years to come until I imploded in on myself and a much-welcomed relief and a sense of peace finally prevailed.

Knock, and he'll open the door. Vanish, and he'll make you shine like the sun. Fall, and he'll raise you to the heavens. Become nothing, and he'll turn you into everything.

–Rumi

2

Life Before the Call to Awaken

As a young child, I was extremely sensitive, and I felt the pain of others deeply. I was very aware of my surroundings and myself, even as a baby. I walked early, and I was talking intelligently by twelve months old, whereby I could hold a conversation with others. As I was conscious of everything as a baby and a child, I have memories of many events and happenings from my childhood.

When I was four to five years old, I noticed and felt immense love within my being, particularly when I started primary school. I thought everybody felt this love as it was who I was. It was what everyone else was too, but they didn't seem to comprehend this and appeared to be disconnected from it.

However, children could be so cruel to other children; it broke my heart to watch what often happened in the schoolyard. I tried to help where I could, but I felt helpless most of the time as nobody seemed to reflect or acknowledge the love and connectedness that I felt so deeply. I subconsciously recognised that I knew something important, but I

didn't consciously *know* what I knew. It was frustrating and devastating, and I can now see that this was the period in my life where grief first began to accumulate and build within me due to a sense of separation.

Living my life in this disconnected way was totally overwhelming, and I felt so alone. Over the course of many years, feeling this sense of separation from everyone and everything caused me an enormous amount of pain and suffering, and it unconsciously gathered in the depths of my soul. The grief that accumulated from the sense of separation continued to gather within me until I married and left home to make a life of my own. But even then, the unresolved grief remained with me and lay dormant, forgotten but often felt. I can only describe it as a deep sadness that created a sense of unhappiness within me. It just lurked in the background of my subconscious and often made its presence felt as it patiently waited for a time to be released.

From my birth to about four-and-a-half years of age, my family and I lived for a period of time with both sets of grandparents. They loved me immensely; I could feel it, and they had no problem showing it. I adored my father's mother and my mother's father; they were two very special people in my life until they passed away much later. Until this time, I found much comfort and solace in their presence, for which I will always be truly grateful.

My Pop had the energy of a Buddha and a well-rounded belly that fit the description perfectly. He showed me unconditional love and compassion, and I felt his love so deeply. We had a beautiful heartfelt connection, and it was reflected in his eyes. His passing was my first human experience with death; I was about eighteen or nineteen at the time. I had not long had my licence and often visited him in the hospital after I finished work because I knew his health was deteriorating rapidly.

His passing didn't upset me like I thought it would, nor was my reaction how I'd seen others react to the death of a dearly loved one. It felt strange to me because I loved him so much, yet I wasn't reacting like most people would. Somehow, I knew that he was with me, in my heart, so I didn't feel any loss. I wasn't a blubbering mess; I was sad that I wouldn't physically see him again but I felt peaceful with his passing.

I remember inwardly questioning my reaction because it was so different to how other people would react in a similar situation. But I just knew it was okay to feel the way I did, and that I didn't have to feel how others might expect me to.

Nana and I had a different valued relationship than what I had with Pop. We were more similar than we were different, and much of what I have transformed in this lifetime related to the burdens that she unconsciously concealed within her. We spent a lot of time together when I was younger, and I absolutely loved it.

Nan passed when my first child was two. Her passing was a little harder to observe as I was much older and could see the fear on her face and in her eyes. Nan instinctively knew her time had come, and she feared the unknown. I wish that I had the understanding then that I have now; I feel I could have been there at another level and better supported her through her transition.

I was about five when we moved into our own home. As with most families, home life had its ups and downs. I grew up in an

era where children were seen but not heard. This prevailing attitude, which many children of my generation encountered, later caused me great difficulties in speaking up for myself. Fear-based childrearing and education were also the norm, and being a sensitive child, I often felt shattered to the core when I was faced with the domineering and controlling behaviours of others.

My brother and I had at times had a challenging relationship during our younger years. We irritated each other and did the usual bickering that often happens between siblings. He was the annoying younger brother that wanted to follow me everywhere I went, and I tried to escape his presence whenever I could.

The imbalance between my brother and me was reconciled on my wedding day. It happened during the circle that was formed by the attending guests at the end of the night's celebrations. You know, the moment when a bride and groom go around the circle and thank each guest and say goodbye before heading off to begin a new chapter of their life together.

Everything between my brother and me lifted the moment we hugged in that circle. All the resentment I harboured towards him and all the baggage I carried in regard to our relationship miraculously left me as we embraced. For the first time in my life, I felt my brother truly loved me. It felt like he had completed his mission with me, which brought tears to my eyes. I sensed all my suppressed emotion well up in me and knew all was done and completed. From this time forward, I have felt gratitude for the role he played in my life, and I now have a beautiful connection and unconditional love for my brother – one that I never had as a child.

Throughout my childhood, I found it very hard to comprehend why life was the way it was and struggled to understand human behaviour. On the other hand, I always knew there was a deep and abiding power within me that would see me through everything. It gave me strength and perseverance whenever I needed it.

In the era where I grew up, physical punishment was the disciplinary norm, but this form of punishment devastated and humiliated me. It was totally incomprehensible in my mind to harm another human being in such a way. Physical punishment reinforced a sense of disconnection, and I also recognised in later years that it reflected what I had come to perceive as my own shortcomings. I was and can be so hard on myself to get things right, and I never allow 'wrong' to be an acceptable option. I would unconsciously punish myself with thoughts of not being good enough, or with the thoughts that I'd upset somebody; therefore, everything must have been my fault. If I felt I didn't get it right or that things were not perfect according to my perception or self-imposed standards, I'd unconsciously beat myself up.

Being a sensitive child, I also grew up feeling I was responsible for some people's unhappiness, and no matter who it was that caused their pain, for some unknown reason I always believed that I was the cause of it. I have spent most of my life feeling like it was my job to try and make other people happy or feel better, particularly if they were angry or sad. I have since realised that it is not my responsibility.

As I grew older, around the age of six or seven, my escape from the harsher realities of life was remedied by hiding under my bed or sobbing uncontrollably on top of it. I'd eventually fall asleep, and sometimes I'd feel that I went into a different

state of consciousness. I'd feel myself grow really small, and my room grow really large, until I disappeared into nothing.

I felt so nurtured in that state and loved being in that space. But then I'd have to return to reality, or was it the dream that I was returning to? Whatever it was, I felt loved and rejuvenated after those experiences and ready to face my life and the world again.

As I mentioned earlier, children of my generation were to be seen and not heard, and my voice was shut down because children were not respected for who they were. They were not seen as equal to an adult. Because adults believed this while I was growing up, I was never asked for my opinion. Therefore, I soon realised my opinions didn't matter and what I had to say didn't matter, so I just didn't speak most of the time because I felt that I didn't matter. As a child, I suffered with tonsillitis often, and I believe this was an illness that manifested because of the blockage I had in my throat centre.

I unfortunately took these beliefs that my opinions didn't matter into my adult years. Once I acknowledged this, I spent many years working on myself to bring my voice back and unblock my throat to allow my voice to flow freely. I did a few public speaking courses because I had such a fear of speaking up in any circumstance, and an even greater fear of speaking in public. If I spoke in public I'd tremble, shake and cry; I couldn't control my reactions. All I could do was recognise them and keep challenging myself to overcome them.

As I worked through clearing my throat blockage, I would have dreams that indicated just how blocked it was and how my progress with it was coming along. In one of my dreams, my head was tilted way back, my mouth was open as wide as it would go and I was reaching down with my own hand in my mouth, digging down into my throat.

I began to pull out of my throat all that had been stuffed in and swallowed over many years. There were balls of wound-up synthetic hair, all in different sizes. I reached in and pulled them to the surface, and they were dry, scratchy and compacted, like massive fur balls. Some of the hair came out in long strands, and they just kept coming and coming. Once I'd removed as many of the strands as I could, next came large shards of broken glass, all in different sizes. As I removed them, I remember having thoughts that they may cut me on the way out, but thankfully they didn't.

My throat eventually became clearer and clearer. I have finally cleared the blockage from my throat and found my voice, and I'm no longer afraid to use it.

As a teenager, I found a modicum of independence in a part-time job. I also took up smoking and social drinking on occasion as I felt it gave me some control over my life. I became interested in boys, or was it that they became interested in me? My love-starved self fell for the trap of thinking I could find some love and affection from having a boyfriend.

Enticed by the attention and looking for what I felt was lacking, I felt pressured to give my first teenage boyfriend what he wanted so that I could feel loved and accepted. I was young and naïve and probably taken advantage of by one who was a few years older and wiser.

My first boyfriend, who I was with for over twelve months, broke my heart. I was just thirteen, and he was sixteen, when we first met; although, I looked and acted older than my years.

He was my first love and long-term relationship, and I tried to please him, tolerating far more than I should have. I really struggled with the pressures of being a teenager and constantly tried to please everybody. I was terribly burdened with peer pressure and the expectations from parents, teachers, my boss and friends. I felt torn and pulled in all directions. Everybody placed their expectations and projections upon me, and I struggled to meet them all. I suffered silently within, and I started to lose my sense of self because of my need to try and please them all. Often it left me feeling distraught and devastated, and at such a young age, I was unequipped to remedy the situations I found myself in.

I fought hard to survive those years. I felt like I'd been thrown into a pool of sharks, and all of them were tearing me to pieces. This was, I believe, the point where I totally lost touch with who I was.

After my first boyfriend broke my heart, life felt like it imploded on me. Like most teenage girls in this situation, I didn't think I could survive. I was drowning in sorrow, and my heart felt like it had split in two. The pain in my chest was excruciating. I somehow eventually pulled my self together and remember pleading from within, 'Just put me with the one you want me with. I can't go through this again'. I guess I was unknowingly making that request to the universe/God.

Within the next few months to a year, I met another boy who crossed my path via the intervention of friends. He shyly asked me to accompany him to his workplace end-of-year Christmas party, and we continued to date after that. I was fifteen, and he was seventeen. We have been together ever since, and he is now my husband of thirty-three years.

Dealing with the pain and grief that comes from a sense of separation and disconnection caused me to become a 'spiritual alcoholic'. For many years, my seeking was no different to any other addict who is seeking fulfilment. I was desperately looking for something that was more fulfilling in life. I wanted to free myself from the inner pain, suffering and unhappiness. We all have the same driving force behind our addictions, although we seek different solutions to quell our thirst. The pursuit to quench my thirst instigated the same selfish attributes that all addicts can have. I wanted what I wanted, and I would do whatever it took to get it – even at the expense of another if need be. I manipulated many situations to aid my spiritual seeking.

I had become buried by my attachment to life's experiences over a long period of time, which eventually diminished my awareness of the divine. I became burdened by the layers of conditioning, beliefs and genetic patterning. The same layers that veiled others gradually imprisoned me; I too became limited, conditioned and veiled from my true self.

I now understand that all of my life experiences had a purpose; it was the perfect soil and fertiliser that my seed needed for germination – my spiritual awakening. The connectedness and love, which had felt so absent and buried deep, only appeared to be lost so that it could be found and fully realised again.

I have now come to a point whereby I no longer judge any of the situations I found myself in throughout my life or the people I shared those experiences with – not that this justifies the actions of others as this is something they will have to rec-

oncile within themselves. But I have come to understand we get exactly what we need to put us on the shortest possible route to realising and experiencing who we truly are.

Self Portrait

Born to a world of slumber, pain and suffering,
conditioned, burdened and suppressed
by the baggage of humanity
that's waiting to be addressed.

Bound by time,
awaiting the call for awakening,
11:11 is the code embedded for remembering
the truth of self,
a buried diamond that awaits
retrieval and polishing.

Even angels must forsake their wings to
be born human in the hope that their heart
will once again sing and God-realisations become a reality.

The serpent never fears.
A powerful creature for initiation
rejuvenation, rebirth and renewal,
transformation is the key;
transcend humanity's belief
in a world that is based on duality,
rather than unity.

Home and wholeness is what one desires,
the burning, the yearning,

Kerry Kirwan

*eruption, destruction and disintegration
exposes the truth.*

*Through reflection and introspection,
one is re-born
by the blade of a double-edged sword.*

*Pearls of wisdom,
forgiveness, healing and balancing,
return to innocence,
feminine and masculine
the sun and the moon,
light and dark,
emptiness and fullness,
purity in perception,
honesty and compassion,
the perfection in all.*

*In the centre of one's own temple,
peace and tranquillity are
the inner sanctuary.*

*From within,
the second coming of Christ,
God-realised,
knowing that what one was looking for,
was what one was looking with:
Love.*

Kerry Kirwan

BLOOM & BURN

Grief can be the garden of compassion. If you keep your heart open through everything, your pain can become your greatest ally in your life's search for love and wisdom.

—Rumi

Opening to the Unknown

Soon after questioning my existence in 1989, I began to have strong clairvoyant experiences, which are the ability to see and perceive future events. I also had strong clairaudience experiences, which are the ability to hear via your higher self or divine guidance – it's like hearing your own thought voice in your head and conversing with it. Clairsentience followed, which is clear sensing or feeling, a heightened form of empathy that allows awareness. I had experiences whereby I started to intuitively know things that most would not be aware of or even want to know. This began with minor incidents. For example, I once left the keys in the boot of my car after getting my daughter into the pram to go shopping. As I was walking along the footpath, I heard clearly in my head the word 'keys', like it was yelled at me internally. It was quite loud, kind of like a loud thought, an inner knowing – if that makes sense – and it stopped me in my tracks.

Rummaging through my handbag, I realised that I didn't have my keys. I raced back to the car, and there they were still in the boot. Clairaudient experiences also happened while I slept; I would wake up with a start and a jolt because someone

yelled my name, but there would be no one there. I was given thoughts as though they were my own, which could be quite traumatic, especially if what I was being told was of a tragic nature.

One particular incident will always remain with me. I was at the hairdresser when the thought started running through my head, *I wonder what it would be like to only have a week to live.* I knew that this was a weird thought that just filtered into my consciousness out of the blue. I acknowledged it but just let it pass without consideration as to what it meant or what was intended by it.

The following week I was at home and glanced at the headline in the local newspaper, 'Local Hairdresser Killed'. Shocked, I opened it and continued to read the story; it stated that her car had burst into flames for no apparent reason and ran off the highway. She was unable to free herself, nor were others able to help her from the wreckage, so she died. I realised that the thoughts that ran through my mind the previous week were like a premonition, which now had relevance, and it upset me greatly as this was not information that I considered helpful or needed to be aware of. Thankfully, I have not received messages like this since.

What I unknowingly opened myself up to in the early stages of my spiritual journey attracted a lot of astral level activity and bizarre happenings, which I really didn't understand, and I had nobody that I could confide in about them. Nobody could help me to understand what was happening, so this was a very stressful, turbulent and confusing period in my life.

I found that what I was experiencing frightened others. Although it did, I needed to reassure them that I trusted the process I was going through. I needed to be able to follow my heart and do what I knew I needed to do. After all, it was my life and my choice to fulfil the purpose of the journey that I had embarked upon.

Visions throughout the night started to happen. One in particular that I awoke to was of a large head in the corner of my bedroom. It reminded me of a wizard. It was surrounded by a wispy smoke ring and appeared to be turning its head side to side chuckling at me, probably because it knew it was scaring me considerably. It appeared to be trying to get my attention. I tried to close my eyes to escape it, but I could see it even with my eyes closed, which both terrified and intrigued me simultaneously.

Another vision I had around the same time was like a simply drawn figure, coloured in pastel shades. It reminded me of the images from a very old-fashioned Rider Waite Tarot Deck and was an image of Christ sitting and floating on a cloud with his legs hanging over the edge.

Once I registered who it was, he too began to laugh at me. I remember questioning inwardly as to why he was laughing; of course, I didn't get an answer at the time of the experience. I awoke wondering and questioning what the meaning and purpose of that experience was. An answer did become apparent many years later, and I will reveal the association in the chapters that follow.

One of the most frightening experiences I had at the beginning of my journey in 1989 was waking up during the night to find that my consciousness was present but my body felt heavy as if it were pinned to the bed. I couldn't move any part of it at all. I had absolutely no control nor did I have any bodily function. I couldn't even speak, and I had no idea what was going

on. I just intuitively knew to close my eyes and go back to sleep and all would be fine when I awoke, which it was.

Because of my growing energetic sensitivities, I felt the presence of many entities entering my house at different times. It felt like they came to me to pass on to the other side or into the light. There seemed to be a never-ending stream of them. I felt like my questioning had opened up and created a huge funnel that filtered everything through my home and through me.

Some of what I attracted was a little mischievous to say the least. I would feel small electric shocks at times, and I knew I was being zapped by unseen entities playing games with me. Things were tossed through the air or pushed off bench tops with no apparent reason. When meditating, I would feel my energy centres swirling in all different directions, and I became bombarded with unwelcome experiences.

Pushed to a point of anger and frustration, I decided that I had dealt with enough! I then demanded that all the unwanted entities/energies leave my home. This showed me that it was my choice as to what happened and didn't happen, and if I needed help, I just needed to ask and it was done. Everything seemed to subside substantially after that crazy period.

Looking back now over that turbulent time, I see it as an initiation that I needed to pass through in order to understand the astral level of existence. I needed to confront the fears I had that were related to the occult or spirit level of existence and much of the unknown. When I look back over my childhood, I can see that I definitely had fears about certain experiences and unexplainable events that I had needed to confront as an adult.

While sitting as a passenger on the way home from a channelling session in 1989, I was relaxing and enjoying the bliss of the energy that had filled my being throughout the evening. My soul's energy was expanded far beyond my physical body, and I felt more alive than ever after being there.

During the ride home, I again had an experience of words filtering through into my thoughts. On this particular occasion I heard the thought, *You will walk the earth as Christ did*. At the time, I had no idea what this meant although I now believe that something beyond my conscious mind knew. I never shared these words with anyone. I just tucked them away inside, never to be repeated or even much thought about for many years to come.

When I attended the channelling sessions, those who were healers offered treatments throughout the evening. As I'd never had a healing before, I was thrilled to take up the offer. I was told by one of the healers that my masculine energy was more predominant – information at the time that made no sense to me at all, and I didn't really know what I could do about it either. However, I was to realise much later that the work that I had come here to do did relate greatly to the imbalance between the masculine and feminine energies. As my path unfolded, I discovered ways to bring balance between the two.

The path to awakening I'd embarked upon often times left me feeling lost and inadequate. I was like a kindergarten child trying to attain a university degree. I was a drop that hadn't realised it was part of an ocean; I didn't know that the depth needed to meet the width. Many years would need to pass before a deeper expansion and understanding would come. I slowly learned that clarity came after experience, and confirmation came after clarity.

After a year or so of attending the channelling sessions and working on my inner spiritual growth, an opportunity came for us to move interstate. I was reluctant to leave, but at the same

time I could feel and sense that imminent change was about to happen, both inwardly and outwardly. I felt torn; I didn't want to let go of the spiritual connections I'd made and the path that I was now walking.

I loved the channelling sessions and all that they represented to me. The thought of having to let them go saddened me beyond belief. I knew that I needed to speak with the channelled entity, Ashram. I had to move beyond my fear of speaking up in front of others, and towards the end of the evening I finally found the courage to ask him about my dilemma. He told me that it would be beneficial to accept the offer to move to Far North Queensland and that my path would continue. He said that the change would bring a period of great growth. His words lifted so much weight and indecision from my shoulders.

I had been extremely worried that my journey would end if I were to leave and relocate elsewhere. I knew in my heart that I was totally devoted to the path that I was now walking. All I wanted was the answer to my existential questions, and I would pay whatever price was asked of me.

When the inward tenderness finds the secret hurt. Pain itself will crack the rock and ah! Let the soul emerge.

–Rumi

4

Time for Change and Growth

In March 1993, we moved from Melbourne, Victoria to Cairns, Far North Queensland. My path to awakening continued to unfold with the magic it had begun with. Moving to Far North Queensland was a very exciting time in my life. We spent the first twelve months in Cairns, but I intuitively knew that we were not exactly where we needed to be, so we searched many surrounding areas to find 'our' place. It was lonely at times but also exhilarating to be discovering and exploring all that was new: a new lifestyle, new friends, new location.

The rainforest area of Kuranda seemed to call us there, and it slowly drew us in. This tropical rainforest paradise was to be our destiny. We found the perfect home, a timber pole home, which was exactly what we were looking for. The property just emerged at the end of the street, and the actual land size appeared to be greater than it was. The home was situated on half an acre of peaceful surrounds, nature, palms and tall pine trees that lined the front entrance. Lush green grass surrounded the home to allow light to enter, something we had realised was important when living in the rainforest.

Throughout my life many amazing occurrences and manifestations have been orchestrated, and this move was one of them. All of our relocation expenses were taken care of, including six months rental assistance. To have other expenses taken care of relating to the purchase of a new home, we needed to move into one within a year – by the 31st March 1994 – and we found that home two weeks prior to the cut-off date. Our settlement was that exact date!

Unbeknown to me at this time, my path was one of renunciation. Leaving behind family and friends was one of the first attachments I needed to surrender, not having a home of my own was another, and the next was finding a home by the date we had been given, with only two weeks remaining, I had truly given up all hope and desire for a home by this stage. This incident proved to me to trust in the process and allow life to unfold as it is meant to. We often need to let go of something in order for something greater to take its place.

The path of renunciation involves letting go of all desires and attachments. This sometimes needs to be done physically or it can, in some circumstances, be done inwardly prior to it manifesting physically. I had to be willing to offer up everything that did not bring the fulfilment I was seeking, and many times throughout my journey I was tested. Did I want what the world offered or would I surrender it to find the truth and the answers to my questions?

I was open to new friendships, and before long I'd connected with a person I believe I was destined to meet. The moment Donna's and my eyes connected, I knew we were meant to be friends. I recognised I had a deep soul connection with Donna; it was a knowing beyond words and description at the time.

This meeting was the beginning of a beautiful friendship and an intense spiritual journey together. We shared similar spiritual experiences and assisted each other through the many trials and tribulations that life challenged us with. Our energies blended amazingly, and we rode out our highs and lows and supported each other on a path we were extremely dedicated to.

Within the first week of moving into our new home, I was given the phone number of a lady in the area who held meditation sessions. Her name was Patricia Chong. Initially, I was reluctant to call because Patricia's last name was Chong. I was afraid I may not be able to understand her, having a Chinese surname. Eventually, I talked my now-good friend Donna into calling her. Donna was just as dedicated to the spiritual path as I was and loved meditation as much as I did, so she agreed to call Patricia to get the dates, times and location details to attend the next meditation.

After arranging to meet Patricia, who by the way wasn't Chinese – it was her surname by marriage – Donna and I were excited to attend our first meditation. We proceeded to drive to Patricia's home, but halfway there, Donna realised she had forgotten the directions to get there. I just kept driving. I trusted inwardly and was divinely guided to Patricia's driveway. As I drove the car up her long grey-stone pebbled driveway, I immediately recalled a vision that I had had a few weeks before. It was one where I had been shown Patricia's driveway in the vision prior to arriving there!

I knew this vision was a confirmation that I was in the right place. Upon meeting Patricia, I felt immediately comfortable. I had a sense of being home, and I connected with her instantly.

She was the first person to ever embrace me with a loving unconditional hug, one that touched my heart deeply.

The year prior to meeting Patricia, I'd begun to have many visions, so I couldn't wait to go to bed and fall asleep to see what I would be shown. One particular vision I had was observing the aftermath of a plane crash, although when I was observing it, I instinctively knew that nobody was killed, which puzzled me because usually there were fatalities. I also noticed that it was daylight and to the side of the aircraft were rows of placed rocks, like a wall of them.

In this vision, I watched many people slide out into the water to leave an aircraft that was floating on the ocean. They waited in the water to be rescued; I also observed that most were of an Asian origin. Within two weeks of having this vision, I happened to catch a snippet of the news. It stopped me in my tracks as it was reporting that an aircraft in Hong Kong had overshot the runway and slid into the ocean during a storm. They were showing the exact same footage that I had already seen two weeks prior in my dream vision.

I've since researched the accident, which happened on the 4th of November 1993 on a China Airlines Boeing 747–400. It was Flight 605 and had 396 passengers, departing from Taipei 6:30 a.m. and arriving in Hong Kong at 7:00 a.m. There were no fatalities, and only twenty-three people suffered injuries.

I realised these precognitive vision experiences were showing me that everything played out in life is predestined and has already happened. I have had many significant dreams on my journey, not just dream visions, and throughout this book I will share what I believe are the most important ones. I will also share how I interpreted them.

One such dream that I would like to share is this one. In the dream, I was in a park with many others, watching aeroplanes do acrobatics. They were in the distance and doing some amazing manoeuvrers and formations. Suddenly, one of the planes started to spin out of control and plummet to the earth; it was heading straight for the park and everyone in it.

I instinctively knew to stay exactly where I was, and as much as I wanted to run like everyone else was, I just knew that I couldn't. I wanted to tell everyone else to do the same as me but it was physically impossible to do so. I was feeling helpless because I wanted to assist everyone else but couldn't. I knew if I tried to help, I would not be left unscathed nor would I possibly survive what was unfolding, so I had no choice other than to sit and watch.

The plane hit the ground, and upon impact, it exploded into many pieces that flew everywhere. People were running and screaming in panic; they were hit with the debris and were either injured or killed. It took every ounce of my courage to trust and not run too. I had to just stay put and not move an inch. I noticed that there were only a few of the many people there that had chosen to do the same as me.

As the debris was hurtling through the air, I had the awareness that everything was predestined because I too felt like every piece of that aircraft – like we were all part of the one consciousness that knew everything. Every piece down to the smallest nut and bolt knew exactly where it was going to land, and everything including me had a place to be.

I sat there and watched the debris land all around me, beside me, behind me and in front of me. It passed right on by, only missing me by millimetres. Large pieces of torn and twisted

metal, nuts and bolts etcetera were strewn everywhere throughout the park.

Just as I thought it had all ended, I could see the cockpit flying through the air, with the pointed end facing and heading straight for me. It tested my resolve in numerous ways. I had to trust the process; my courage was to withstand what was happening, and I had to believe in my knowledge. The cockpit hit the ground and skidded along the grass, digging it up as it went. I just sat and cringed and waited for the impact, closing my eyes in anticipation. I thought to myself, *This is it. I'm not going to survive this ordeal.*

My eyes were shut but I hadn't felt anything, so I opened my eyes and looked up. The pointed tip of the aircraft's cockpit was directly above me like an umbrella shading me; the shadow of it encompassed me and was reflected below on the grass.

I found myself sitting in the triangular wedge of space that remained beneath it and the ground, with my hair slightly touching the cockpit. I took a deep breath of relief as I sensed that all had ended. I stood up to make sure that it had, particularly before I moved. I looked around and the only people alive or not injured were the ones who had chosen to remain where they were.

This dream has meaning on many levels. The most significant, I believe, is whatever we are faced with in life, don't run from it. There is nowhere to escape to, so we must remain and face whatever comes our way. What comes our way is predestined, and having the courage to face what that is will eventually free us. Knowing this will save unnecessary pain and suffering.

I always seemed to have certain experiences for a period of time, and when I realised the reason why, they would then pass and something else would be revealed to me. Every new experience would bring me an awareness of the workings of the universe.

During my first year in Cairns, I felt so tired all the time. I was so tired that I thought something was wrong with me, some kind of illness like cancer or something very sinister. My energy was depleted, and I hardly managed to get through each day. It was such a struggle, and all I wanted to do was sleep constantly. It was difficult to sleep and keep a household functioning with two little ones to take care of (I had had my second child by then). I went to the doctors and had some blood tests etcetera, and the doctors said that there was nothing wrong with me. Looking back, I feel that I was being prepared for what was about to unfold once I met Patricia. My energy was being adjusted in some way, and my body struggled to cope with it. So many changes were happening rapidly and on every level of my existence.

Within the first few years of meeting Patricia, I started to have energetic experiences; it was unlike tiredness. I instead became physically incapacitated, and I could hardly function. This feeling would come over me like a descending wave of energy. One minute I was fine and the next I could hardly speak, think or function. I had to either lie down if I could or I'd just sit and wait for it to pass. It would go as quickly as it came.

This would happen at any time of day or night. It would happen anywhere and anytime without warning. I'd just feel it coming over me. It wasn't an unpleasant experience; I did enjoy it. It was possibly how one would feel if they took drugs and were high and in an altered state of consciousness. Although this is just a guess as I've never been one who's taken drugs. But it was like my energy was being utilised somewhere else, and it stopped me from fully functioning wherever I was at the time. These moments only lasted between five and thirty minutes. I just accepted what was happening without question, knowing it would eventually come to pass.

Every human being is a guest house. Every morning a new arrival. A joy, a depression, a meanness, some momentary awareness comes as an unexpected visitor. Welcome and entertain them all! Even if they're a crowd of sorrows, who violently sweep your house empty of its furniture, still, treat each guest honourably. He may be clearing you out for some new delight. The dark thought, the shame, the malice, meet them at the door laughing, and invite them in. Be grateful for whoever comes, because each has been sent as a guide from beyond.

–Rumi

5

My Teacher, My Master, My Greatest Reflection

Patricia held meditation sessions periodically throughout the week, and I attended these over many years. After meditation, she shared mystical traditional spiritual stories. They carried a particular energy relevant to what may have been occurring at the time. The stories had a deep meaning; usually a meaning that couldn't be understood intellectually as they were more symbolic in nature.

Sometimes I could feel what the stories related to and their meaning, and there were times when I couldn't or I was in a space where I heard them but was not conscious enough to comprehend their meaning. I was okay with that if that's what was happening; I knew that being there in Patricia's presence was all that really mattered.

I attended as many weekly meditation sessions as I could. Patricia also allowed me, along with others, to have a one-on-one session with her by appointment. I did that often, at least once a week if I could. I did both meditation and personal appointments with her for many years.

After only a few months of meditation, when I was sitting privately with Patricia, she said some words to the effect that made me think she knew me inside and out. She knew and was aware of my deep inner longing, my sense of not belonging and the pain and suffering that was hidden deep inside of me.

Nobody had ever acknowledged that about me before; no one had ever even noticed my unhappiness. Not even I had been able to give expression to it – it was just something I lived with. Much of my past was now tangled in the present. Different scenarios had played out, but they all related to the same struggles and themes that had been repeating throughout my whole life.

The acknowledgment made that day by Patricia, I believe, was a divine initiation, and I was bestowed with a gold Om that I treasured and wore around my neck for many years to come. An Om symbol embodies divine energy, and it has three main characteristics: creation, preservation and liberation. Om is all-encompassing; it is the essence of ultimate reality and unifies everything in the universe. Its sacred sound is the vibration of the universe. Om is derived from Hinduism and is considered to have high spiritual and creative power, helping us to connect with our divine selves.

I unconsciously, although willingly, placed my trust in Patricia. I had always been one to only rely and follow my own inner intuitive instincts, and this was definitely one of those moments. She knew the deepest longing within me, and I presumed that she knew everything about me. I feel I let my own will be somewhat put aside as I surrendered myself to her presence. I believed that this was what I needed to do as I felt Patricia knew more than I did, particularly in relationship to the journey that I had just embarked upon. Which she did because she had walked the path before me.

I don't believe Patricia ever took advantage of the situation. I feel Patricia always had my best interest at heart, and she never did allow me to become too overly dependent upon her.

I still utilised my own inner instincts and wisdom to guide me through what I was experiencing over the years that followed. These instincts helped me do what was required to free me from the limitations that bound me. Patricia's presence always occupied the vastness that lay beyond everything – the presence of God.

I loved being in Patricia's presence, and I instinctively knew that she would become one of my greatest teachers – one who I later realised didn't teach anything – although her presence drew me closer and closer to her until we became one. I didn't realise what was happening at the time, but I trusted my intuition and continued year after year to attend the meditations week after week. The pull to be at these meditation sessions was so intense that I could not have resisted even if I had wanted to. It was like a drug that I just had to have no matter what, and I would do whatever I had to do to get it.

Listening to the snippets of Patricia's life story intrigued me; periodically, she would share aspects of it and the many facets of her spiritual journey. Patricia shared that she met her teacher in Hawaii, whose name was Divine Mother, and she was connected to the lineage/energy of Rama Krishna. Divine Mother was a quaint, unassuming Japanese lady whom Patricia, along with others, spent many years with while devoted to their spiritual path.

I felt very much in the inner circle of Patricia's meditation group. After a few years, we began to travel to different over-

seas locations and connect with others who were also part of the meditation group. I always accompanied Patricia along with a small group of other meditators. We travelled to Brunei, Borneo, Singapore, Germany, Malaysia and Myanmar, and some countries we visited on more than one occasion to keep our connection with them established. As time went by, the group that travelled also grew; sometimes, there were up to thirty or more or us.

It was difficult to explain to family and friends the reason I was drawn to this path and the work that I was doing on the inner levels of existence. It wasn't logical to anybody else, and trying to make it logical made me look like I was crazy because I couldn't explain it. I had to trust that being in Patricia's presence regularly had a purpose and that I had been divinely guided there for a reason, one that I hadn't yet fully understood.

I was extremely fortunate that I didn't have any idea of what that purpose was, and that I had no comprehension of what was about to unfold within me and my life. What was about to unfold was extremely challenging and intense. Patricia's presence and the energy she transmitted packed a punch. It was transformational and quickened the process of my awakening beyond belief.

Patricia played many roles in my life; one of the most important was holding the space for me to merge more fully into my own true presence, of which hers was the reflection for me to see, acknowledge and finally accept. For that to happen, everything that masked the true essence of my being was stripped away, layer by layer: conditioning, beliefs, attachments, unresolved fears and emotions, everything that created an egoic self – a separate self from the truth. The process was unrelenting, and it took great courage, will and devotion to continue on the path I had chosen.

When I had my one-on-one sessions with Patricia, I did not like to go there with too many questions. I always allowed her to speak to me so that I could absorb everything she had to offer, even if I didn't understand it intellectually. My mind seemed to empty before I got there, and even more so in her presence, so there were no questions to ask anyway. Although I'd think of many the following day that I could have asked, but this was just my mind returning to its usual chatter and enquiries.

Weeping at the end of each session happened often because my mind had no comprehension of what was actually taking place in the depths of my being. This did not deter me, however, and I still kept showing up. The sessions we had together were very intense, and I could feel the transmission working within me. Sometimes I'd need to go home and sleep as I'd be exhausted after most sessions. I often released emotional residue either by giving expression to it verbally in discussion with Patricia or it would leave my body energetically and/or physically via my nose and eyes. They constantly leaked tears and mucous throughout the sessions. I'm sure I looked like a total mess, but I allowed it to happen regardless.

Throughout my time in Patricia's presence over the years, I intuitively felt when it was time to outwardly release more and more of what she represented to me. I felt that Patricia also simultaneously recognised the same. I also believe that the higher intelligence that decided this was beyond our apparent physically separate selves.

Somewhat reluctantly, I accepted when these periods came. Something within me knew it was time to let go of her more and more. As much as I felt comfortable with the attachment, I knew I had to relinquish it. It happened very gradually over a long period of time, years actually. The best way I can describe it is like breastfeeding a baby to sustain them. In the beginning, they are given all they need to establish everything that is required to build a strong foundation for them. Then when the time is right, they are weened more and more. This weening happens gradually so that it may be noticed but it's accepted easily. Over time, babies come to realise and accept that they are transitioning and are strong enough from within. Eventually, they are no longer dependent on breastmilk for their sustenance. I knew from within when it was time to finally let go of my last remaining attachment to Patricia. I did it voluntarily, but it wasn't easy to do.

Separating from my great teacher meant withdrawing from everything and everyone that had meant so much to me. Letting go of her also meant letting go of the meditations and most of the friends who gathered there, the overseas trips and the sense of feeling that I belonged somewhere. It was one of the hardest things I had to do, but I knew I had to do it.

Once I had made this most difficult decision of my life, particularly in regard to renouncing Patricia, my actions were questioned. People said to me, 'Don't you know who she is? How can you just leave?' I did know who she was, and I had come to a place where I knew who I was, so I had to integrate that.

A baby can't be fully weened if they continually have a breast tempting them to suckle. So I knew I had to allow myself time to adjust to not having Patricia spiritually nourish me. I had to nourish myself from within and become strong and independent from all that I had been dependent upon.

I'd had a dream prior to this happening. In this dream, I was surrounded by all my meditation friends, and we had just finished a meditation. The group was beginning to disperse, and I could feel myself lifting off the ground. I didn't want it to happen, and I inwardly pleaded, 'Please not here, not now, not in front of everyone.'

But it kept happening; I knew I couldn't stop it, so I just went with it, lifting higher and higher in front of them all. As I lifted, my arms also lifted, lifting me higher and higher until the ground and people below became so distant. My arms spread further and further apart until they could no more, and then suddenly Christ and I were one. I felt like a giant cross in the air. As soon as I acknowledged this, I descended back down to the ground. Nothing was said, and I just brushed myself down, straightened myself out and walked away.

I had noticed that when I had attended the meditations, I would already be sitting and waiting for most of the others to arrive. I could feel that an energy worked through my being to clear the room and also clear the energy of those who were arriving. I was naïve to this for a very long time; it was something I only realised after a friend who attended the meditations made a comment to me about what he experienced. He said he came to meditation not feeling that great, but then I'd be there, and he felt my presence transform the energy within him and the room. Once this was bought to my attention, I became very aware of the energy that transmitted from my being.

A subsequent similar dream revealed my healing presence within the meditation group. In my dream, we were all sitting in a circle preparing for meditation. As meditation began and

everyone closed their eyes, I found myself levitating above the group. I was levitating over the inner circle just above each person in the circle. I passed over each person; I could feel that I was one with Christ and his healing energy. The energy that was transmitted either came from my hands, my heart or my eyes. Each person was given what was needed, and most were unaware of what was occurring.

One morning after meditation, I had an unusual experience with the same person who noticed how my being transmitted energy. We were chatting when all of a sudden our eyes locked together. In an instant, my eyes seemed to swallow him up, and he was taken into the emptiness and spat back out again. It was not at all anticipated, and it was only a few seconds that had passed for the whole experience to be complete. Needless to say, it took us both by surprise.

We didn't really speak about it when it actually happened. I think we were both in shock and didn't know what to say. I became a close friend to this person over the years, and we had even more amazing experiences together that I will share in later chapters.

After leaving the meditation group, I kept contact with a few close friends. I didn't have any contact for many years with Patricia, although knowing we were one from within sustained me in the years that followed. Everything else except my family held little value in my life next to that.

The years that did follow were not easy; some of what I experienced was amazing, although I went through some very dark periods. At times I could hardly function. I slept a lot, and didn't see anybody or talk to anybody except for my immediate family. There were times I did hear from and see extended family members, and I could hide what I was going through inwardly for short periods of time.

At times, I had no drive to do anything; nothing in the world interested me. I'd been in dark places before but this was by far the worst. The emptiness just swallowed me up, and I didn't have the strength to fight or resist it, I just had to accept it. I'd gone beyond caring about what was happening.

Set your life on fire. Seek those who fan your flames.
—Rumi

6

The Work

(While still in Patricia's presence)

My dreams throughout my journey were an important element that I became more and more familiar with. They were a tool that I used often to bring clarity and understanding to the situations I was faced with. I utilised them to understand myself and others.

I often dreamed of different homes. Upon entering these homes, I would notice their neglect or state. Sometimes dust was layered upon absolutely everything, and the house was filled with cobwebs or looked like it had been unoccupied for some time. I knew it was my task to clean it but it felt so overwhelming. My initial thought always was, *Where do I even begin?*

I had many similar house dreams that followed over the years, and these homes represented the work I needed to accomplish to get my 'house' in order. The house was a symbolic representation of my body and my mind. Some rooms needed

to be cleaned whereas others required relocation or renovation. And some were just crazy constructions that you could not even imagine.

A huge transformational process was taking place. It was what I most desired, and I knew that I would do whatever it took, no matter how painful or how much work was involved. I knew that no one would do it for me, so I was totally prepared to do the work because I somehow knew it was more painful to not do it and remain ignorant.

Prior to leaving Melbourne and relocating to Far North Queensland, I had seen a fairy shop and had just loved it. Inwardly, I thought to myself that I would love to create a shop just like that one day. But I didn't give it a second thought.

I was delighted to discover that once I had settled in my home in Kuranda in 1994, the thoughts of a fairy shop resurfaced, and I realised this was going to become a reality. I wanted to create and open a fairy shop of my own!

After sharing my thoughts with a neighbour, they told me that the landlord of some new shops in town was looking for a business owner to create something special in one of the shops for rent. Kuranda was a popular tourist destination. I instinctively knew this was where my fairy shop was meant to be.

Once I had realised it was a fairy shop that I was meant to create, I inwardly asked one morning while lying in bed, 'If I'm to own a fairy shop, what will it be called?' Immediately, the divine stamped the name in my mind, and I felt the word 'Spell Bound' impress all at once across it. I was in such shock that I nearly fell out of bed! I loved it! The name was just perfect, so now I definitely knew *what* I needed to do. I just needed to figure out *how* to do it as I had never been in business before. I had no idea where to begin; I had to trust that I'd figure it out, and of course there was some divine intervention that took place.

I required stock for the shop, so I looked on the Internet and found that there were gift trade fairs that I could attend, and there was one soon to be happening in Sydney. Because my business wasn't quite formed, I felt a little apprehensive and fearful that I would not be allowed to enter as I had to supply proof that I was a business owner.

The next minute, to my surprise, my home phone rang. The person on the other end was a male and asked if I was starting a business and hoping to go to the Sydney trade fair. I told him that yes, I was. I was astonished by how he knew, and more surprised at how he had my phone number. He said he was from a company that was displaying products there. He told me if I happened to have any trouble getting into the fair that I should ask for him. He was there as a representative for his company and stated that his name was John Love. John assured me that he would assist me if I needed him to get me into the fair. I thanked him and hung up the phone. Totally confused, I wondered how he knew to call me, but I had no answer, so I just let it go. This reassurance made my decision easy: I was going to the Sydney trade fair without any more fear or trepidation about it.

As luck would have it, an extended family member was keen on my idea of opening this business and became a partner in it. I felt some trepidation about having extended family move to Cairns for the business as I had lived quite freely for the past year or so – without too many distractions, expectations or family obligations – except for my immediate family. I won-

dered if this was going to change and if I would be able to continue with my newfound way of living life. However, I also acknowledged that this would provide an opportunity for me to work on deeply rooted ancestral issues.

I proceeded to go to the trade fair and was allowed entry without any difficulties. I was in my element and loved gathering the products that I felt would complement the shop. I then came to the stall from where my phone call originated from. I asked the stall attendant if John Love was available to talk to as I wanted to personally thank him for helping me with the decision to attend the fair. The woman's response was that she had never heard of him. Miracles do happen, and the divine works in mysterious ways at times!

I opened the fairy shop, and initially it was quite stressful as I tried to juggle being a working mother. My business partner was yet to relocate so I sought help instead of pushing myself beyond what I was not capable of doing. I didn't want what I was doing to be at the expense of my wellbeing or our family – so I could see that I'd grown and transformed some of my previously limiting behaviours. I was beginning to find better ways to live a more balanced life. I had begun to honour and love myself.

Soon after this, I also started to really open up and show affection to others – something that had always been a problem for me since birth. I had felt that keeping my distance from people would protect me from getting hurt or taken advantage of. Earlier on in life, I had realised that it was easier to give up expectations of receiving unconditional love and acceptance from others – only to be crushed by disappointment when these expectations weren't met.

When I understood it was me who had to initiate change, particularly in regard to showing and giving affection, I resisted, but something in me knew if it wasn't me, then who? It had to begin with someone, somewhere along the family line in order for change to happen. I felt like a real fake at first but I persisted until it felt natural. I came to understand why change is resisted as patterns and conditioning are extremely hard to transform. It was not easy at all to choose another way.

Many issues were deeply imbedded into every fibre of my being that were previously hidden from my conscious awareness, but all were related to personal and collective conditioning. I decided it was time to give to others everything that I expected from them. I felt immense resistance to change, but I continued with it. I gradually observed that giving love to others actually freed them to be more expressive, and it transformed their unconscious behaviours. They too were then open to giving and receiving love and affection in ways that they previously hadn't.

I was eventually able to break through the many patterns that conditioned me, especially the fear and control patterns, aspects that had been subconsciously running my life. I was able to recognise the moments that I was operating from these patterns and then chose another way. I realised that I didn't need to control things; they would be perfect by allowing and trusting that they would be. Because of the inner work that I did in confronting my own fear-based and controlling behaviours, people developed a newfound respect for me. As I changed, my relationships changed for the better. This was because I had come to perceive that others were a reflection of the aspects that kept me from experiencing who I truly was.

When I changed from within, others automatically began to behave differently to reflect that.

I felt so light, free and very empowered; finally, I did not fear confrontation or conflict with others. I had grown enough and had found the courage to confront the ones who reflected my limitations. Symbolically, they had become monsters in my psyche. I feared these monsters immensely, and by doing so I gave my power to them. I knew I needed to slay them to free myself as they had kept me captive for far too long. When the time was right, I drew back my sword and was not afraid to use it. It was either fear imprisoning me or fighting for my freedom. I chose to free myself from the monsters within my psyche, which others had become a reflection of.

Once I'd cleared the reoccurring pattern and conditioning of fear and control, I was given confirmation, again in the form of a dream. This dream helped me to understand how far I'd grown in regard to personal relationships. It was also reflective of the relationship that I was working upon within myself, and more importantly, it was the closure that I needed to move further along my path of awakening to inner unification.

This dream occurred in 1999. I was travelling on a bus, and I knew that I had a task to complete. The task was important, so I hopped off the bus that I was on. As I got off this bus, I knew that it would never be possible to get back on it. After getting off, I wandered the streets aimlessly until I came to a large and mostly empty warehouse, which I entered. I meandered around inside until I noticed there were a few packed boxes. I walked over to them and sat down on one, not knowing what to do or where to go. I had nothing and I was nothing, which was freeing, so I just sat and waited. I didn't know what I was waiting for, but then I heard the handle rattling on a door that was close by. I looked over to it not knowing who or what was there. The door opened, but I sat unmoving, not knowing what to expect.

When the door opened, my first reaction was fear. My stomach dropped when I realised who was at the door; our eyes met and my heart began to pound. This person was someone I had feared all my life, although they looked to be a younger, brighter version of themselves. They proceeded to walk over to me, and I stood in anticipation, fearful of what was to come because of my past conditioning.

However, this person held out their arms out to me. I was surprised and relieved. We hugged, and as we hugged, we had an appreciation for each other that we had never had in our earthly life together. But in the dream, we had such a deep soul connection. We both acknowledged that we had fulfilled the part we had chosen to play in each other's lives, and all that remained was a deep love and respect for one another. I came to accept that all earthly relationships have purpose – our pain becomes a cure.

Totally devoted to my path and the work I needed to do, I started to look at everything that created a reaction within me. Life always managed to construct situations that evoked what I most needed to reconcile. I learned very quickly that it was never about the other person; they were only playing a role that allowed me to see what I most needed to acknowledge. This then exposed what was limiting my greatest potential.

My higher perspective could also be applied to my past so that it too could be re-assessed and reconciled. Much of the past was now tangled in the present. Different scenarios played out, but they all related to the same struggles and themes that had been repeating throughout my life.

BLOOM & BURN

One afternoon a customer entered my fairy shop right as I was about to close down the door at the end of the day. He was a short, well-rounded middle-aged man with a very wispy up-turned moustache, not my usual customer. I was extremely tired and knew that I still had to go home and continue with household duties.

He started to question me about different spiritual topics, but it was my choice to engage or not. It was also my choice to tell him that I was finished for the day.

I bit right into the feeling that I should remain and speak with him as there was a reason for him to be there. I was sure I could share all my knowledge and help him in some way, which I proceeded to do.

After spending a good forty-five minutes or more of my time with him, sharing what I knew by answering all his questions, he turned around to me and said, 'I already know all that you have shared with me, I was just testing you.' He was quite smug with himself and had a smirk on his face as he turned around and proceeded to leave my shop.

I felt so violated by him although I admit that I allowed this to happen. I couldn't stop crying; I sobbed and sobbed, and at the time I didn't even understand why I was crying so much over the experience. It was like I was a huge bubble of water that he had come in purposely to pop, leaving me with the aftermath. I felt like I had been hit by a sledge hammer. In the coming days, I accepted that this experience had totally shattered my spiritual ego, something I hadn't even realised I had.

During my journey of awakening, there have been many great masters and teachers that I have had the privilege to merge with energetically. I have integrated the essence of what each of them represent. What an amazing blessing to have: divine grace. I am very grateful and appreciative to all who have assisted me on my journey, no matter their level of existence or what role they have played in my life here on earth. I do not ever judge the role of another or the scenarios within my story as every experience and person has been as important as the other. All of us are a like a facet of a diamond and the whole diamond simultaneously.

I went through an extremely intense period in my life that lasted many years before it came to a completion, which related to integrating the essence of the Buddha – emptiness – and the renunciation of everything. The lead up to this period and the integration of this energy was tremendously challenging. I will share the experience in detail with you later in this chapter. This period in my life was very taxing for me on many levels because there were multiple processes happening concurrently and consecutively.

During the integration period, many challenges arose within my relationship, particularly once I met Patricia. My husband and children helped me to remain grounded and anchored me to this earthly level of existence. Although this existence felt restrictive at times, I also recognised its importance. I didn't always understand what I was going through as most of what I was dealing with was activated internally and was dealt with on the inner planes of existence. It was not easy for others to

comprehend what was happening as there was no apparent reason for my emotional reactions. They often confused me too.

I'd periodically enter dark nights of the soul and sometimes thought I was going crazy. My mind did not want to let go easily; it wanted to remain in control and would do anything and everything to sabotage my growth. The layers that had formed upon my being were peeled back, wounds were exposed and everything that I thought defined me was burned away in a fire that was all-consuming and unrelenting.

I was not aware at the time that Patricia's presence was that which fanned the flames – as were life and the experiences I was having. I'd go through periods of unbearable intensity. All my fears, beliefs and conditioning had to be acknowledged for what they were. It was an extremely painful process that my immediate family was part of and witness to, and they tried to support me as best as they could.

My relationships evoked what I most needed to look at (that which needed to change and be reconciled within me) and many times I wanted to escape. I didn't want to have to face what was being provoked within me. I felt I had reason to run if I was angry, resentful and miserable, although I never did. Something in me knew that this was not the answer and that there was no escape. I had to face what I had to face, so I did. I knew that resistance only caused more pain and suffering, even though it was something I sometimes did unconsciously.

I finally came to a place where I felt the intensity of my relationships with others had lessened somewhat. I'd been through what seemed like the worst of it all. I had always felt very supported in my marital relationship in all ways – together we navigated the ups and downs that life challenged us with and respected each other immensely.

However, I was at the fairy shop working away when intuitively I knew that I had to tell my husband that our marriage was over. I didn't understand why I had to do this; I had absolutely no reason at all other than I was being inwardly instructed to do it. I was beside myself with even the thought of having to do this. I felt absolutely nauseated and knew it would be shattering; I didn't want to be the one to do that, not now.

Later in the day, as time went by, I was tormented more and more by the thought of ending my marriage. How could I do such a thing, the kids will be there, how can they not be affected by it, how can I do that to them? Inwardly I questioned and pleaded, 'Don't make me do this, not after everything we have been through together.'

Intuitively, I knew I had to do it. I knew that I had no choice; it was part of my spiritual process. My path, as previously mentioned, had been one of renunciation. This too was seemingly one of many things I needed to renounce and offer to the divine. I had to renounce my husband, my children and my status as a mother and wife. I also remembered the words that I stated before leaving Melbourne all those years ago: That I would do anything that was asked of me to answer my questions: Who am I and why am I here? Little did I realise that it would be my family that I would have to offer up. At the time, I felt like I had given up everything, except them. I'd let go of every worldly attachment and desire I had.

Even prior to this renunciation, I could sense the presence of a soul waiting for me to decide if I would bring it into this world or not. Because I could feel its presence, I asked for this being to communicate with me during a meditation. During the meditation, the soul spoke to me and said it would like to taste

the world when it ripened. This confirmed my awareness of its presence as I knew these were not spoken words that I would ever articulate. Willingly, although torn inwardly, I decided that I did not want to become pregnant and have another child. I renounced the third child that I had always planned to have. My desire to know and realise the divine was more important to me at that time, and I did not want anything or anyone to delay that realisation.

But back to the dilemma of renouncing my marriage. During that day, while processing my confusion, Patricia happened to drop by the shop with a friend. I didn't need to say anything to her; clearly, she could see I was upset as my eyes were welling with tears.

I will never forget her words. She said that life is not about a happy family. Then Patricia left my shop for me to consider this statement and for me to accept that ending my marriage was what I had to do when I went home.

After speaking to my husband about my decision, I was totally emptied and shattered by what I had done. I then called Patricia. She was the only person I knew who would understand my predicament. I asked her if I could spend the night at her place as I didn't know what else to do. She said to come over. I was beside myself by this stage and was in shock. I felt like a car windscreen that had just been shattered into a million pieces, and Patricia had just tapped a piece of it out and the rest came tumbling and crashing down into a pile of rubble. After spending a little while at her place, confused and tearful, the next minute all I remember her saying to me was, 'Okay, you can go home now, unless you do want to stay here for the night. You can if you want to.'

I felt numb. All I could think about was what my family had just gone through and what I had been put through. This was total craziness. I was on the brink of a complete breakdown and felt entirely destroyed. I'd done what was asked of me and now I was to go back home like nothing had happened. I was utterly traumatised and exhausted, and I felt completely emptied. Nothing was left. This final act of renunciation (even though I didn't actually have to renounce my marriage in the end) was the end of the driving force from within that had forged my path for so many years.

The culminating point of this renunciation experience was actualised and confirmed for me on the inner planes, again through a dream-like experience that explained what I had been through. I find dreams can summarise an experience in its fullness, and they also give confirmation through symbolism in a way that I can personally relate to.

In the dream, I was waiting with anticipation outside a room for an initiation process to begin. I was not the only person waiting; there was another with me who had gone into this room before me. After a long period of time, he was carried out by two men: one at his feet and the other holding him under his armpits. This person was teetering between consciousness and unconsciousness; he was totally exhausted. Whatever he went through was all that he could withstand, and it made me feel more than apprehensive of what I was about to experience.

My turn to enter the room had come, so I took a deep breath and braced myself. I knew it was not going to be easy. I was invited into a room, and I intuitively knew there was another room to enter beyond it. But I would only be allowed to enter it if I passed the test that came with the first room.

I stood waiting in anticipation for what was about to come. The next thing I knew, two gargoyles appeared in the room. They approached me, grabbed me and began to fling me across the room, slamming me from one wall to another, smashing me from one side to the other. I was in total shock. I was not expecting this. At first, I stiffened and was afraid and rigid. I had resistance, and my inner thinking even tried to pull out the drawcard, *I'm a female; you don't do this to females*. I soon realised that this was beyond being male or female – gender had no relevance in the matter. It felt like the pounding was never going to end; I was exhausted, and the gargoyles were unrelenting.

I was thrown around the room over and over by both of them until I fully surrendered to the process; I totally gave up fighting them and their methods. I had nothing left to offer them. I totally surrendered, and there was no resistance left in me at all. It felt like nothing remained, like I'd been emptied of everything. Once the gargoyles were satisfied that their work had been accomplished, they stopped and let me pass through to the next door into the adjoining room.

This was a room of Buddha consciousness. It was a welcomed relief after what I had just experienced. I too was utterly shattered and exhausted just as the person before me. Although I had the strength to walk out once the initiation had been completed.

It took me some time to assimilate the experience, but a new way of being emerged over the coming weeks. Within my physical reality, I became more content within myself and with life. I was no longer seeking, and the inner longing subsided. My marital relationship dynamics changed for the better, and we each moved to a new level of independence while still remaining together. I had always unconsciously resisted life, especially the lower levels of existence, as they have always been painful for me to embrace and accept. The fact that I was resisting caused even more pain and suffering. I finally understood that I couldn't ever separate myself from any level of existence – all levels had to be embraced and accepted unconditionally. All of it was reflective and helped me to embrace and realise who I was. Nothing could be excluded, but everything that I had been identified with had to be surrendered to reach this state of being.

At another level, this particular dream initiation related to the driving force behind my seeking that I had previously mentioned – whereby I felt like I shooting star – a star that ignited and rocketed across the universe until it eventually imploded on itself and became a black hole. The driving force, the desire to know myself, the meaning of existence and the unrelenting pull from within finally came to an end when I gave up everything and completely surrendered. All the veils had to be lifted or renounced, including my attachment to being a wife, a mother and having a happy family.

After this dream, I was aware that only one thin veil remained. It was such a welcome relief. Finally, I felt a sense of peace and calm from within. Once the driving force was fully exhausted, the implosion happened and the energy transformed. I was no longer an energy force that emanated light; I had become a black hole, a vast emptiness that drew all close to it into itself. All of the inner intensity had dissipated, and the driving force had imploded; finally, it had all ceased and this was such a relief.

To digress for a moment, I'd like to share some information on black holes. While chatting with a close spiritual friend, she

questioned me about the universe and my understanding of black holes. I responded by saying that there is only one black hole, although there appears to be many. I told her that this perception can only be realised and is dependent upon being able to pierce a hole through the veil of all illusions, or by passing through an existing black hole. That opening then leads to a vast empty space where nothing else exists. Although perceiving from the other side of the veil where everything appears to exist, there are many openings that can be observed. From this perspective, everything has the potential to experience no-thing if it comes close enough to be drawn into the opening that leads to the vastness.

This phenomenon, I believe, is an outer reflection and is symbolic of the process that takes place for those who want to experience the truth, realising who they are by going beyond all illusion to where no-thing exists.

We can achieve this awareness for ourselves, but the path is not for the faint of heart. However, if one is lucky enough, we can be drawn to another who has attained this state of being. Their presence will enable a seeker who comes close to them to be drawn into that vastness, which is exactly how a black hole functions. I believe that this analogy describes how one becomes a spiritual master, and black holes are symbolic and representative of all the great masters that have walked/walk this earth. Their presence alone will draw what appears to be others into their company for them to realise the same, and the phenomena of a black hole within the universe is the symbolic reflection of their state of being. It represents how they work.

On rare occasions, two black holes can merge. This is called a binary black hole. I wonder if this is the reflection and a symbolic representation of when two great masters on earth meet and merge and become one greater opening into the vastness of no-thing? When two black holes are close to one another, this is the orbital period. Gravitational waves can be felt, and this stage is called a binary black hole in spiral as they will merge as one, particularly once they are close enough. Once this now single black hole settles down to a stable form through what is called ringdown, any distortion in its shape will dissipate. In the final stage, the black holes can reach an extremely high velocity. Space-time itself is distorted and dragged around by the rotating black holes as the gravitational wave amplitude reaches its peak. The most recent detection of this process happened in September 2015 and was announced in February 2016.

It has been difficult for me to share many of the experiences that I have had with others. My experiences were often a culmination of many different experiences and were not yet perceivable in their entirety. So, at times, it was a lonely journey, although I would never change a thing about it.

Meanwhile, my fairy shop, Spell Bound, went from strength to strength. I loved bringing my creative expression into reality. From the outside, the shop looked like a magical, glittery castle. The inside was scattered with fibreglass trees sporting dried tree limbs and imitation leaves for foliage. There were misty mountain backdrops painted on the walls, a full moon and a canopy of fabric on the ceiling like a circus top tent. Lashings of material gathered into its centre, colours of blue, mauve and

purple. All kinds of mythical creatures resided within the shop's walls, which were made by the many talented people who became our regular suppliers.

We had a storytelling cave that children loved to have their picture taken in, sitting on the many toadstools with the gold, sparkling, dotted purple velvet cushions scattered on its floor of dried rainforest leaves. The roof of the magical cave had optical fibres that changed colour and sparkled like stars in the night sky.

Spell Bound allowed me to connect with my inner child, and it allowed many others to do the same. Many would come to see what had been created, and the shop had a beautiful energy that was often noticed. People came just to bask in and enjoy what was on offer.

Sundays were always my busiest day of the week. They were market days, and tourists flocked to the area. One particular Sunday was special as I had one of the most amazing experiences of my life. A young man who looked to be in his mid- twenties wandered in and asked me if I had some time to share with him. I had no idea who he was but I intuitively knew that I had to sit with him.

He only wore a pair of baggy shorts, no top. He was slender and had very messy hair. I especially noticed his deep, dark penetrating eyes. We sat in the cave at his suggestion, and he held my hand, slouching back comfortably into the dried leaves scattered around on the floor and propping himself up with a cushion. The young man started to speak in a language I didn't understand, so I told him so. He replied in English that I did know what he was saying; he was speaking Hindi language, which I intuitively knew, just not its meaning.

I accepted what he said and just listened. He did at one point begin to speak in English again and questioned me about my understanding of the symbolic meaning of the sun and the moon. I didn't really have an answer at that moment as it wasn't something I had ever contemplated.

We mostly sat gazing into each other's eyes, which was something I was used to doing as I had already spent many years with Patricia, and that was something we did together often.

As he spoke, I noticed something small rolling around in his mouth. The young man said that he had something for me, but my reply was that I needed no enticement to keep me on the path, and I politely declined his offering. I presumed that whatever was rolling round in his mouth was what he was going to give me if I accepted it. After the experience, I often wished I had accepted the gift. Then I would have known what was rolling around in his mouth as he spoke.

Only days before this strange encounter, I had watched a documentary on Sai Baba and how he gifted his followers by the giving of material objects that he materialised out of nowhere. I had never desired such gifts nor did I require them or anything else external to entice me to seek the truth. I would unequivocally seek truth regardless of any offering. I didn't feel that there was a choice for me; the realisation had already been made, so I just had to align with it.

After watching a program on Sai Baba, however, I consciously acknowledged the existence of other amazing teachers and masters. I previously hadn't comprehended their purpose and that they were among us. I did not ever think for a minute that one may visit me. I believe the greatest gift that was given

by my visitor was the energy transmission as we sat together and gazed into each other's eyes.

I had only spent about ten minutes with this young man, but I had felt his stillness and the comfortableness that he had with himself – a lack of self-consciousness, I would say. He left my shop after he spent a little longer by himself in the cave, and when he was ready, he wandered out into the arcade with many dried leaves stuck to his back. He hadn't cared about these at all.

As he left my store, within a minute, I felt drawn to look outside and see if I could see him wandering down the arcade. He was gone almost instantly and was nowhere to be seen. I was surprised as I did expect to see him, but it was like he had evaporated into thin air.

Over, the next few days he kept popping into my consciousness. I kept an eye out for him, but I did not see him around town nor did he come back to the shop. We were a tourist town and many travellers came and went, which was what I thought he might have been.

A week after meeting this man in my shop, I felt compelled to go to a Friday night meditation that Patricia held at one of the other meditator's homes. I never usually went to these, but this particular week I did. There were many portrait-like pictures on the wall of the home where meditation was being held, and I was drawn to look at them.

One picture in particular held my gaze. The face was so familiar. All of a sudden, I got this massive slap on my forehead and immediately the image on the wall and the image of the man in my shop from the previous Sunday merged within me.

I asked the meditation host whose picture this was. She mentioned it was Babaji, and told me a little about him. I was in total shock. Without sharing my awareness with anyone, I realised Babaji was the one I had sat with in the cave of my fairy shop.

I couldn't wait to find out more about him. I read that he is an eternal great master who can appear anytime and anywhere around the world, and he has taken on many forms over thousands of years. Babaji is written about in Yogananda's Book, *Autobiography of a Yogi*. Babaji had visited Yogananda on many different occasions throughout his spiritual journey. Sri M is also another that he has visited, who described his experience to be much the same as what mine was.

Eventually, I came to deeply contemplate the symbology of the sun and moon many years later. I ultimately understood why it was so important for me to know the symbolism of the sun and moon, and that this was obviously why Babaji was questioning me about it at the time of his visit. I realised that the sun is symbolic of the masculine, while the moon is symbolic of the feminine. A portion of the work that I came here to do was to assist humanity and myself in relationship to the unification of these two polarities

I achieved this unification personally and collectively; my ancestral line has been purified of the imbalance between these two forces. I have shown that it is possible to achieve a higher state of consciousness while partaking in ordinary, everyday life. I did not realise this when I spent that moment with Babaji. I guess at the time he was preparing me for the work and that realisation. Remembering this experience and what was spoken about was the confirmation of what I had achieved once I'd completed the work.

Babaji is connected to the linage of Jesus Christ, and so too is Yogananada; they are a few among many other great masters of

the same linage. Christ consciousness is the highest state of consciousness that one can attain spiritually; once achieved, we are completely immersed inwardly and outwardly in God's presence. In order for this to occur, the masculine and feminine energies must be united.

There were many pinnacle points on my journey where I had other realisations and direct experiences that related to Christ consciousness and God via dream-type visionary states. In one visionary experience, I found myself rising up higher and higher, and the higher I went, the faster and faster I sped through the atmosphere. Stars whizzed past me, and I began to spiral. There was no sense of a physical body anymore, only conscious awareness remained.

I then passed through light and knew that I was going to meet God. I remember feeling so surprised and very excited; I wasn't expecting to meet God. Wow! Finally! I came to understand that one of my deepest unconscious desires was going to be fulfilled. It was totally unconscious because until this experience happened, I hadn't known how important meeting God actually was to me.

All of a sudden, there I was in the stillness looking at myself, my own hands wrapped around my face so lovingly, and my face beaming back at me in awe. I was God looking at me – it was so discombobulating and unexpected.

A similar experience relating to God happened again not long after the previous one. I was driving down the Bruce Highway from Kuranda to Cairns and was in a deep thought conversation where I randomly conversed with an inner aspect of myself.

I was contemplating God and all of a sudden, the penny dropped. I realised that God and I were one, and that was what my experience of meeting God was all about – my previous experience was clearly showing this to me. As I made this realisation, a euphoric feeling came over me that passed from my head down to my toes. I turned into golden light; all sense of myself disappeared while driving my car down the highway.

What little awareness of myself that remained didn't even care that I was driving down a highway and that I could run off the road or crash at any moment. Basking in the golden light felt so amazing. I chose to go with the feeling and accept the consequence of that. Before I knew it, I came back to my senses and my body. I was still driving and continued on to my destination, completely astounded at what had happened and that I was still alive.

After I had made the acknowledgment that we are all one and that we are all divine, I willingly, although sometimes reluctantly continued to do the work required by taking responsibility for each issue that arose in my life through the encounters I had. If I saw something other than the divine in somebody else that pushed my buttons and evoked an emotional reaction within me, then it was a veil I needed to lift that was hiding and limiting who I truly was. I knew that what I was clearing were my personalised imbalances and also those that had collectively accumulated from previous generations, which are one and the same. I came to understand that every person in my life was there to assist me on my journey. They all helped me to recognise my self-imposed limitations and move beyond them.

I will be with you in the grave on the night you leave behind your shop and your family. When you hear my soft voice echoing in your tomb, you will realise that you were never hidden from my eyes. I

am the pure awareness within your heart, with you during joy and celebration, suffering and despair.

—*Rumi*

7

The Wounded Feminine

As a baby and a child, I felt like a fully-grown woman who didn't want to be naked or exposed. Being naked brought up such anxiety and absolute fear and panic in me that I could not explain. It took years, probably around forty of them, for the depth of this behaviour to finally unravel and completely rise to the surface of my conscious awareness so that I could release it.

In this chapter, I will share how this fear unfolded in my life and what was buried so deep within my being. Layer upon layer surfaced to reveal what this fear and terrifying reaction was related to, which I will conclude in Chapter 12 with an even deeper realisation that surfaced while writing this book, relating to the same issue.

As mentioned above, I was born with an issue as a baby – I had a huge fear about being naked and exposed. I did not allow any males or strangers to see me naked. The only people who I felt somewhat comfortable with being undressed in front of were my mother and grandmothers.

Being exposed brought up such fear in me, but I never knew why it did, and I didn't know that it wasn't a normal way to behave. This fear came in with me at birth.

I lived my childhood and teen years not thinking too much about it and was unaware it was such a huge issue that would eventually have to be resolved. I always kept myself covered; I hated undressing in front of others, especially at school events such as swimming, sports days or my friends' sleepovers.

As a child, when faced with certain situations where there was nakedness or exposure of genitals and no adult supervision present, I would inwardly freeze and be filled with fear and unable to move. Other kids just laughed and joked and thought nothing of it. I didn't know why I had the reaction I did, although I now know that I was afraid of being in a position where I could be taken advantage of sexually.

I had always struggled with sexual intimacy, although when older I sometimes participated reluctantly or to please another. I often found myself in situations that I did not feel comfortable with, where men forced themselves upon me. This negative behaviour was drawn to me repeatedly throughout my whole life, through various experiences that I often drew to myself, without knowing why. I take full responsibility for some of the situations that I did allow myself to get into, although I drew many of the negative experiences to me unconsciously and for no apparent reason at the time. Eventually, this brought me to a point whereby I had no choice other than to ask why.

I'd always had an unconscious aversion to men that became more and more apparent as time went on. I feared that they may misinterpret friendliness and kindness to mean something more. Sometimes I avoided conversations with men unless I knew them really well. I was always conscious to not send the wrong signal if I was interacting with a male. I'd never touch a male in a kind gesturing way; I wouldn't offer friendly touches of affection under any circumstance in case it was misinterpreted. Although, I always did dream of finding the perfect man to live happily ever after with.

Sexually, I was always very self-conscious, and I avoided intimacy of every kind where I could. I never knew I had a problem; I just thought it was the way I was. I even noticed that when I hugged anyone, my fists would be closed as they rested behind their back. I eventually realised that my closed fists were a symbol of holding back love, and it was so hard to open them. I eventually forced myself to do it and to get comfortable with doing it, but I couldn't understand why it was so hard for me to do.

Being close or intimate with somebody brought up so many unconscious reactions and emotions in me. I had a mountainous blockage to overcome and was entirely unaware of its cause. Later, I realised that the conditioning and expectations on women of my generation – to get married in white and be a virgin on our wedding night – sent a clear message to my subconscious that sex before marriage was wrong. I grew up feeling that sex was taboo and was not acceptable to have.

Being openly naked in a familial setting was also taboo, and as a female child, I was always expected to behave like a lady. Even exposing underwear was not acceptable. This too reinforced my incarnational belief that nakedness and the human body was something to be hidden and fearful of and to avoid at all costs. I never knew what it may evoke if I were seen to be in a vulnerable state of being or what may happen because of that.

The deeper I moved into my awakening journey, the more I started to understand that a lot of my awareness arose from

interpreting situations energetically, and I had to trust that what I received in this way was valid. Issues could then be brought out into the open or exposed. This was something that I had previously felt I couldn't do because I was speaking or revealing what most people thought was hidden and not accessible. I also believed that if I spoke about such things that appeared to be hidden then those things could be denied and not accepted. So for most of my life, I had made an unconscious choice to refrain from revealing what I felt, which denied an aspect of who I was, as well as the truth hidden within and behind situations. Once I acknowledged what I had been doing, I soon changed that pattern.

When it came to intimate relationships, these created many energetic battles, which were all fought in the subtle energy realms within myself and were reflected by others. It was at times overwhelming and exhausting. Once I recognised what I needed to do, the energy struggle was finally able to shift into a more mutual energetic exchange with another. Eventually my intimate relationships became more about connection than getting a desire met. I felt like woman who was valued in her own right – a woman who was able to choose to connect intimately or not; this was not the case before.

I have always been energetically sensitive; I feel and sense personal and global events way before they actually happen. I am particularly aware of sexual/lustful energies. I acknowledged at different times that I had been sexually violated on an energetic level by certain males who had crossed my path, particularly once my spiritual journey began. At times, I became so angry because it kept happening, and it continually triggered many emotions from within me that related to the wounded feminine, exposing that which was dormant and unresolved.

I eventually broke down and cried, asking the universe why I kept drawing these situations to myself. My whole life I had been taunted by these same issues relating to men, sex, anger, resentment, repulsion, men groping at me, wanting something from me, taking advantage of me. It just never left me alone. It followed me everywhere, and I couldn't escape it; my issue was always reflected back to me in some way by an experience with a male. All of it continually prodded me to confront a hidden dormant issue that I was yet to realise.

At least I'd now come to a point of finally asking why and finally recognising there was an issue, one that had been unconscious for so long. It was baggage that I didn't want to carry anymore. I intuitively knew that if I didn't address the issue and get to the bottom of it, I would be physically raped at some point in my life.

I came to understand that within each of us, the feminine has been denied to varying degrees. There is a wounded feminine within all of us, whether we are male or female. Her wounds stem from all types of abuse, particularly sexual, as many have taken advantage of her, abused her and disregarded her needs by suppressing her. She is in pain; she is wounded and extremely angry and resentful that she has been disrespected. Who she is and what she truly represents needs to be acknowledged and integrated in order to heal the wounds of her past. All that's been repressed and suppressed has to be accepted, forgiven and released. My life's experiences continually brought all of her pain to the surface for reconciliation. In Chapter 8, I have detailed to the qualities of the feminine as many of her attributes have been denied and have not been utilised as they were intended to be.

The awareness that came from my own experiences gave me an understanding that has helped me greatly to see from another's perspective, particularly when my own issue in regard to the wounded feminine started to unravel. I understood why others may do what they do and disregard another in the process. Sexual pleasure can be very addictive and extremely hard to control when it's derived from an instinctual, primitive level of existence. Seeking sexual pleasure once it's desired can be a desire that can overtake and control one's whole being and actions, like any other addiction. Strong desires for orgasmic release can in some cases override morals and behaviour and hurt another if they are not a willing participant.

Sexual energy in its primal state of desire has an almost uncontrollable intensity driving it; it can be an addiction that can easily override purer intentions in order to have its needs met. It's a bit like having a devil on one shoulder and an angel on the other. Which one's voice will be the most convincing? Which one's instruction will be followed? Can the desire be repressed or redirected or will it be expressed to have the desire met?

Fulfilling sexual urges by disrespecting or taking advantage of another can be easily justified in the moment. Often remorse may arise in the one who didn't follow what was moral or acceptable, but it's too late when another may have been taken advantage of or even abused, particularly if desire was not controlled in the moment. Especially if the desire was too compelling and given in to for one's own pleasure at the expense of another. Because I could see from this perspective and was able to grow from my own experiences, it helped me to forgive others and myself for perceived wrongs. We have all played the roles of victim and perpetrator, personally and collectively.

There was also a period where I practised as a massage therapist for a few years. It was something I would never have imagined nor seen myself doing, particularly because of the issue that I needed to resolve. Although I now see that this period was beneficial as it was something that helped me to overcome my issues connected to men in relationship to my wounded feminine. I distinctly remember my first paying client – a young man. It was his first massage ever, and he was petrified. I intuitively knew he carried an issue similar to mine. I felt his fear and his vulnerability. As I began his massage, I smiled inwardly and felt privileged that he trusted me. I realised that we all have our crosses to bare. I enfolded him into my presence and knew he too needed some unconditional nurturing and acceptance in order to heal himself.

It took a considerable amount of work and dedication to the process to unravel all that had created my unconscious behaviour and reactions regarding the wounds that I carried forward from birth. Particularly in regard to my inner female, for which men, sex and being naked evoked all the hidden unresolved pain. This issue that I was burdened with created such conflict within me, but its reconciliation is what enabled me to reunite my inner masculine and feminine aspects.

The culminating point of my issue eventually came through my willingness to embrace the repulsion, rage and resentment that sexual intimacy had been evoking in me for so long. I allowed my body to tremble as tears seeped silently down the sides of my face onto the pillow. I felt deeply every painful emotion that was rising to the surface of my being without resistance. I knew everything that I'd been working through was the preparation for this moment. I had to stay with it until the

end. I had to release completely all that was coming over and through me.

While this was happening, I sensed a bright white light in my forehead. I focused on that as it was all I could carry forward with me; everything else had to be released within that light with absolutely no emotional residue remaining from the experience. As I focused on the light, I perceived that I was not myself. I was a young African–American Negro woman, and I was being raped. I knew I had been repeatedly raped by the white male I could sense upon me. He was the master who owned the slaves working for him on his property, and he used me over and over to have his sexual needs met. I was fully conscious through the whole experience.

I suspect that this experience was possibly similar to past life regression under hypnosis. However, it was something I had never experienced before in such detail. I realised that this was the unresolved issue that I had brought with me into this world as a baby; it was that initial unresolved experience that had been further layered upon, emphasising the imbalance between the masculine and feminine within me. I had had no recollection of this lifetime at all until I allowed myself to fully embrace everything associated with it and layered upon it. It had affected nearly every aspect of my life. I had to dig back through every layer that had accumulated upon it until the root cause could be acknowledged, resolved and removed.

Universally, there is an imbalance between the masculine and feminine. It is both collective and personal – the masculine has dominated, and the feminine has been repressed, but it is a condition that we can change and transform. Equality and balance can be achieved. A divine marriage from within is possible, and unification will end all conflict.

I worked diligently over many years to reconcile and release the deep-seated wounds of the feminine, the initial African–American rape experience and everything that had been layered upon it. I did it for those before me and for those who will come after me. I know that my grandmother on my father's side carried the same imbalance within her, as do most women, but her issues related to the same issues that I needed to re-live and release. Unfortunately, she was unable to recognise where her imbalance originated from and wasn't able to reconcile her issues in regard to intimacy and the wounded feminine in her lifetime.

Often I would meet my grandmother in dreams when I had cleared aspects of the ancestral psyche that related to her. We would meet and embrace in those dreams and sit and chat. I also felt her presence with me when I was struggling; I would speak to her inwardly and tell her that I was doing this for both of us. I can also see that the wound has been resolved for all the females that will follow in my genetic lineage.

I had come to realise over the years that when I watched movies that evoked a strong emotional reaction in me, then it was highly likely that there was something within me that I needed to work through and release. Movies can expose some of the unconscious issues that we have identified with.

Movies or programs that were love stories always left me heartbroken, particularly if they didn't end well. I'd always cry or sob, sometimes embarrassingly so. Deep down this was my greatest longing to be unified; it's what I thought marriage and loving relationships represented. The stories expressed and exposed what I most unconsciously desired: I wanted to feel whole and complete. I'd been conditioned to think that I could

achieve that by meeting and merging with another. I hadn't realised that it reflected what I needed to do from within.

Love stories evoked the pain of separation and exposed the unresolved grief that stemmed from that. I carried so much pain and grief because of living life here on earth surrounded by unconscious, disconnected people who reinforced that sense of separation.

When I watched movies where African–American Negro women were raped and African–American Negro men were tortured or killed, I would sob uncontrollably. I'd feel rage and repulsion, and this would be mixed with disgust and heartbreak. I chose to avoid watching such programs; I couldn't put myself through them. Although, if I had to view something of that nature now, I could watch it and not be as emotionally caught in the story because of the work that I've done.

A dream I had especially relates to the completion of the work I had been doing with unifying the masculine and feminine energies within. I was led into the woods and taken through an opening between two large trees. There was a cleared allotment of land that had a country homestead on it with a large veranda surrounding it. I was led up to the steps and through the front door. As I stepped into the entrance, the door was already open and ready for me to enter. As I entered, I noticed the walls had been beautifully carved from timber; they were carved with everything in life I could imagine.

I was in awe of the beauty these carvings offered. I was taken into each room of the house; each was as beautiful as the other. I was then led into the last room, a room that was very unusual because it was in the centre of the house, and every other room in the house surrounded it. As I entered into this room, I instinctively knew it was my room. It had been completed with the most beautiful woodcarvings from ground to ceiling. As I looked up, my eyes were immediately drawn to a carving of Christ's head, which was in the centre of the wall directly in front of me. It was the most predominant carving among all else that had been carved on that wall.

As I continued to look towards the top of the ceiling, which was the tallest point of the house, I noticed what looked like carved organ pipes from about three-quarters of the way up on each of the four walls that led to the ceiling. There were open gaps between each pipe that allowed air to flow freely through into every other room in the house. The room felt so sacred and still, and it was the most peaceful room of them all. It held a blessed and holy atmosphere within it.

I eventually left that room after acknowledging all that I sensed and observed, and I was led out to explore what remained. As I was about to leave, I passed the two that were detailing the home – a male and a female working diligently together. They were the ones carrying out the carvings upon the walls. They were working meticulously and painstakingly to create and carve the perfection that was evident upon these walls. I noticed that their task was almost complete; they had only a little way to go before they were back to where they had begun.

The dream was symbolic of the completion of the work that I did in relationship to the masculine and feminine; my inner masculine and feminine worked harmoniously together until their task was complete. The entire house represented my whole being, and it had been transformed in the most beautiful way possible. The room within the house that I knew to be my room, which had Christ's head carved at its centre, was also in the centre of the house and opened to every other room. This room is representative of my heart and its openness to everything. I now love unconditionally. When the work was completed, balance and harmony had been restored, and I attained Christ consciousness, which I had had as a small child but just didn't realise it back then.

In the midst of the darkness, a moon appeared with its brilliance. Stepping down from the clouds, it glanced at me. Like a skilful falcon that hunts a bird and steals it away, it captured me and flew back to infinite space. As I looked for myself, I could not find me, for my body had become all soul in the tenderness of love. The nine spheres of heaven dissolved in that moon as the ship of my existence drowned in the sea of love.

—Rumi

8

Myanmar and the Twin Flame Journey

My inner 'thought' voice was at it again; a knowing rose up from within, and it questioned me on how I would respond if I were to have an encounter that evoked a strong, loving connection with another man. My unconscious thought response was that I didn't really know. I then wondered why I was having such thoughts and let them go. I was married and had never looked or hoped to find anyone outside of my marriage; I had never felt the need to.

I then proceeded to have thoughts about my first teenage boyfriend. Back then, my brother had been a kind of chaperone for me when I was dating. I can now see that he was unconsciously fulfilling his role to prevent any monkey business from happening and was there for my protection to ensure everything played out in my best interest. However, I hadn't realised this back then and tried to ditch my brother as often as I could. This was detrimental as it put me in situations that I wasn't old enough to make decisions on – I only thought I was. So I certainly made decisions that were not in my best interests back

then. I felt this awareness now gave me insight to trust and accept circumstances as they are and not manipulate them to be otherwise. The reason for this awareness to surface would soon become apparent.

In 2002, I was invited to go to Brunei and Myanmar with Patricia's meditation group. It was our first visit to Myanmar. We had been to Brunei on several occasions as there were spiritual connections there that we had previously established. Through that connection we were introduced to a lovely spiritually devoted lady that we call the 'Burmese Mother'.

Our trip through Myanmar was made up of a small group of eleven travellers from Australia, Brunei and Myanmar. Myanmar had just started to allow tourists into their country. We were excited to experience all that it had to offer and looked forward to meeting the Burmese Mother. We were embarking on a tour that the Burmese Mother had helped to plan; it had been organised prior to us arriving. The trip was going to take us to the many sacred sites that she had suggested we visit, and she, her husband and her son would accompany us on our journey.

I was completely ignorant about what was going to unfold throughout our journey, which made it all so much more amazing and exciting than I could have ever imagined. I had such a connection to this country; it was a land filled with simplicity and untouched beauty. Everything flowed as we travelled the country landscape, passing through many small villages on winding, dusty potholed roads that were lined with all kinds of animals. I noticed pigs, ducks, chickens, dogs and cows that were all roaming freely as if they belonged to everyone. There were even lizards grasping tightly to tree trunks. I noticed the tiniest details as we travelled and I gazed out of the bus window.

I observed the beauty and kindness of the many unassuming people who spent their days relaxing, working, meandering and travelling in all types of rickety old vehicles, including horse and cart. All of it touched my heart so deeply. As I gazed from the bus window, I felt my eyes connect with many of the people who lined the streets of the villages we passed through, and I felt their unspoken love and acknowledgment of me. It felt like I were them and they me; there was no separation between us.

My heart expanded more and more as my eyes welcomed the feast I received as we passed through each remote village on our way to Bagan. I could feel from the pit of my stomach an immense energy surging up and through me, pulsating up to my chest – my heart was expanding and aching with the pain of love. With that came deep sobs for a forgotten past; tears flooded my eyes and streamed down my face. It was overwhelming, irrepressible and something I hadn't ever experienced before.

The energy continued to come and go in waves as we persevered onwards with our travels. The further I travelled and explored this unique country, the more I felt like I was home. Something hidden deep within me was being activated that I was not conscious of.

As I went through my experiences, I could see that Patricia was also going through her own and was connecting deeply with the Burmese Mother. There were times of immense intensity for her. I noticed that she was struggling to remain conscious and was not always fully present. I assisted her where I could but there were many times I felt that I couldn't

as we both seemed to be going through something transformational, simultaneously. She too was in the process and a completion was occurring for her: The unification of knowledge and devotion.

A MEETING OF EAST AND WEST
(Patricia's personal account of her union with the Burmese Mother)

We call her 'The Burmese Mother' – a gentle, humble housewife who has dedicated her life to Buddhism by meditating eighteen hours a day, with one hour walking and one hour sitting: A Devotion practice we in the West could not emulate.

A first meeting with this soul took place in the hotel lobby of a Yangon hotel – a meeting that brought the extraordinarily emotional union of one from the East and one from the West. Unable to speak each the other's language, we embraced in tearful, sobbing hugs, like siblings who had shared a womb, sensed but not known the other.

DEVOTION or PROFOUND DEDICATION*: A further visit to Myanmar and the opportunity to be guided by one who, through her years of meditation practice, has acquired gifts of 'seeing' life in a continuum that spans many lifetimes. This allowed those of us who shared the journey to not only learn of the relationships and revisit places that had been lived in other times, but to begin to experience what the true meaning of 'Devotion' is.*

This visit brought the sharing by several of us, in a meditation that ceremoniously wrought a merging of we, who represented the 'West' (Knowledge) and those who represented the 'East' (Devotion).

Since this time, there have been other pilgrimages to the place once known as Burma, where the land, with its myriad of temples and stupas, is steeped in the Devotion of the Ages.

Guided and edified by the fruits of Devotion personified in the one we call the Burmese Mother, we of the West have come to experience its meaning and have had the opportunity to nurture the growth and the flowering of the seeds of Devotion that reside in each of us.

P. Chong

During my trip, I was overcome with love from the Myanmar children. While we were waiting for assistance after our tour bus broke down, a group of children between the ages of six and fifteen came running over to the bus and stood at the window beside me. The bus window was covered in dust but the children were looking at me intently and smiling, mouthing to me through the window that they loved me. Their cheeky little faces peered in and vied for my attention. I felt overwhelmed in the most beautiful way imaginable.

With their tiny fingers, a few of them started to draw love hearts in the window dust and write the words I love you, pointing to me and mouthing the words 'I love you' again and again. I felt flooded with indescribable love and joy.

I was amazed at the synchronicity of this experience. How did the children know to write and say such fitting words to me in that moment? Many other people were on the bus that day, but they chose to come to my window.

The children were not requesting anything of me; they were just giving what they had to give unconditionally and, in that moment, they chose my window to engage with and share their love through. Once the bus was fixed and we were on our way, they ran alongside it still engaging, waving and blowing kisses.

We finally arrived in Bagan and discovered a beautiful hotel to stay in that overlooked the banks of the Irrawaddy River. It was such a serene area, peaceful and majestic, and the energy was all-encompassing.

Bagan is a spectacular Buddhist centre scattered with over two thousand 9th to 12th century pagodas, temples and monasteries. Many are complemented with fine wall paintings, monuments and sculptures representing the dynasties and successive kings from past cultural and religious life.

During our first evening's meditation in Bagan, I found that I went easily into a deep state of consciousness without realising it. Towards the end of the meditation, my awareness returned, and I knew I was in the hotel room although I could hear bells ringing, chanting and chimes, which I felt were coming from the grounds that surrounded the hotel. The surrounding grounds were dotted with ancient pagodas and temples.

I could feel the presence of a time when the area was truly alive; it was like a market place, and an assortment of animal noises echoed in the distance along with the hustle and bustle of a bygone era, all aligning with the present moment. I suddenly realised that I was experiencing this, and that it was all happening within me, it was a past moment aligning with the present moment, a culminating point of the perceivable – two being one. This was very symbolic of what was about to unfold.

I felt so connected to this land, but also felt like I had no feet and floated rather than walked. It was difficult to remain grounded, although I was unaware that most of the time I wasn't. I was divinely intoxicated, basking in bliss and enjoying every moment that was offered. Bagan was soon going to offer me something even more profound to experience, and it involved one of my travelling companions – a lovely man I had previously met through our meditation circle.

I had first met this man in 1998 on the night of my thirty-third birthday. I celebrated this birthday because it was a pinnacle year for me, especially in regard to my spiritual seeking, or more to the point, the end to my seeking. I wanted to celebrate that aspect more than my age. Instantly, I felt a connection with this man's soul, although I didn't understand at the time how deep our connection was. I just knew he was a beautiful being; his sparkling blue eyes caught my attention as they were so clear and bright.

But back to the present day in Myanmar. Once we reached Bagan, our tour bus took us to the ancient pagodas. As we travelled on the bus, I found that I was sitting with and chatting to this same wonderful man. We had never really spent any extended time together, so this was an opportunity to get to know each other.

While exploring Bagan, we found ourselves in front of a huge golden Buddha statue. Both he and I stood in front of the statue in awe of its beauty. Unbeknown to us at the time, this moment initiated what was about to unfold between us.

When we were back on the bus, an energy between us activated. I felt like Pandora's box popped open inside me, and as this happened, l became intoxicated by love. I was feeling all

kinds of sensations from within. We could both feel it, but I can only speak of my own experience.

After another short lunch stop, I got back on the bus and sat next to Patricia. Images arose within my inner third eye. I saw an image of a phallus, and my entire being was pulsating. It felt like an indescribable ecstasy that I'd never experienced before. I was able to know this man's thoughts, even when I wasn't next to him. At that moment, I couldn't separate his energy from mine, and we felt one and the same. I had no idea what was happening and why. All I knew was that it felt amazing but at the same time it was all very confusing.

One evening after dinner, this gentle man and I sat in the garden area and did an open-eye meditation. It felt like our energy spiralled together so delicately, dancing and entwining forever upwards and uniting as one. We didn't need to speak verbally; we spoke without words, energetically.

After our meditation, he said to me that he had seen me as a beautiful divine-feminine goddess. I only felt his energy clairsentiently (I feel more than I see). During our meditation, I recognised him to be representative of my divine masculine aspect. Once I acknowledged this, I made a conscious choice to see him as myself, a reflection of my divine masculine energy.

I acknowledged the love that I was feeling was rising within me, although it appeared to be linked to someone external. I knew I needed to acknowledge that; I intuitively felt that it would be a trap and a mistake to see it as something external to myself and seek it outside of myself. I knew that the experience required integration and acceptance from within.

During the rest of our travels, whenever this man and I came close to each other, it was overwhelmingly magnetic. Something ignited, and our energies automatically blended together. It felt amazing, like every atom of my being was alive, dancing and free. I felt limitless expansion and totally naked, not literally, just that there were no veils hiding who I was. I felt more of who I truly was than I had ever experienced before.

There were times when I actually felt embarrassed by the energy that had activated between us. It was a huge magnetic field that surrounded us, especially when we were in close proximity to each other. My energy field felt huge – it felt like enormous love – unconditional love, divine love. We both enjoyed the experience that each of us evoked in the other; it was not wrong. How could something that felt so amazing be wrong? Pure love can never be wrong. It was not happening for the purpose of cheating on or hurting another. It was not instigated by either of us. It just happened and couldn't have been prevented, and we couldn't have stopped it from happening. The connection was beyond our personal doing; it was divinely orchestrated.

We also had a chaperone. One of our travelling companions was with us constantly throughout the whole experience. I trusted that he was there for a reason; it was something that I'd been prepared for previously with the inner discussions I'd had prior to the trip, mentioned earlier in the chapter. I believe that our experience was not to be taken to a physical level, nor did I have the desire to do that.

This journey for me represented love – love in its highest form, a pure love that I had not acknowledged in this way before. I believe it was the result of all that I'd worked so hard to reconcile within my being: the unification of the masculine and feminine. This was reflected to me throughout the whole jour-

ney. I felt it permeate my entire being, flooding me completely from within and without.

Before we left Burma and after a meditation at the Burmese Mother's home, she did a ceremony and blessed a tiny piece of silver for each of us and gave it to us as a gift. I felt inspired to give my piece to my male friend, possibly because I had the unconscious awareness that it was going to be difficult for him to process and understand all that had happened.

I bought him a silver chamber on a leather cord necklace so that his and my silver blessing could be contained together, representative of what we had experienced. I felt that the gift was an outer symbolic representation of what needed to occur from within, that each of us were a symbolic aspect and together we were one, even if we appeared to be apart. The necklace represented the integration of the masculine and feminine, that which allowed divine love to be experienced.

I eventually integrated the experience over a long period of time, and continued on my journey, a journey that was not always comfortable, although I seemed to navigate my way through the turmoil, confusion and dark periods that often arose on my path.

The years that followed my Myanmar trip were at times extremely challenging. My family and I had already moved from Cairns to Brisbane in 2010, and I had relinquished everything that had meant so much to me. I felt like I was floating in a large cavernous abyss, empty of everything, with nothing to grasp on to, nowhere to be, nowhere to go. It felt like this passage was never-ending. I had touched on this cavernous space briefly throughout my journey but never for this amount of extended time.

I knew that I couldn't resist the experience. I had to fully accept it and try not to escape or distract myself from it. It felt like days on end of pure blackness – all desire was gone, all motivation was gone, and I was alone most days. Connecting with others was almost non-existent.

There was nobody to share my experience with; I instinctively knew that nobody could help me through this period. I couldn't go to a doctor as they would only want to label me as depressed and offer me a prescription. I knew I just had to accept where I found myself with no resistance whatsoever to what I was feeling and what was happening.

This was such a juxtaposing place for me to be in. I had always been one to use my will to drive and push forward relentlessly, no matter what, but this time I couldn't. I felt totally flat and burned out, there was nothing left of me, let alone my willpower. I had to unequivocally embrace and be the space that remained when I was no longer there. Once I came to this realisation and accepted it, the space was actually enjoyable. There was no longer any resistance, everything was comfortable and peaceful – the darkness, vastness and aloneness became my inner sanctuary.

Fast-forward to March 2018, and I found myself boarding an aircraft with my former Cairns meditation group, excited to be once again reconnecting with my spiritual family and travelling to familiar places that I hadn't been to for so long. I have some very close friends in Brunei and was fortunate enough to catch up with them again.

My heart swelled with joy and gratitude to be once again present with them. During a lunch gathering with many that I hadn't seen in such a long time, tears rolled down my cheeks. I didn't think anybody noticed, but before I knew it, Patricia was in front of me and touched her forehead to mine. In that instant I felt immense love, and my heart expanded. I was totally limitless for a brief moment in time, and I knew I was once again where I belonged.

I instinctively knew that this trip was another opportunity for my for dear male friend/twin flame to finally embrace and acknowledge his inner feminine and integrate it within himself. I did what I could to assist with his process as the energy between us will always be embracing, magnetic and all-encompassing. During this trip, we came to learn that we are twin flames and connected to the 11:11 sequence (which I will elaborate on later).

My twin flame and I have shared some amazing experiences; some of them are still integrating. We will always be in each other's heart no matter if we are together or separate as we are one. This is something that I wrote after we returned from our journey.

Divine Union

A child of God, pure and innocent,
A peaceful warrior who's driven to seek,
Here to bridge the connection between mortals and gods.

Prepared to answer the call from Source, that which is balanced and contains all contradictory elements. Born to unite all that is hidden, suppressed and conditioned.

Kerry Kirwan

A painful process of purification, destruction and resurrection.

Guided by inner strength and wisdom, driven by the yearning for intimacy and connection, absolutely devoted to transformation and integration.

It's a call that can't be ignored.

A burning desire for unification, the pain, the ecstasy, the delicate entwining of inward lovers, completing the merge to birth a Divine Marriage and the consummation that inevitably happens.

Intoxicated by the expanding magnification, it's an intimacy like no other, purified by the flames of passion, naked, unconditionally attracted, lost to what appears to be one another.

(11:11)
It's time to accept and realise the source of all reflections; it's time to integrate the divine masculine and feminine to finally experience the power of true love.

It's a time of completion; it's the end of pain and suffering and all the conditioning that comes from separation. It's the grace that's bestowed for responding to the call.

Through vulnerability and devotion, a closed off heart will open, Christ consciousness, a timely resurrection of the purest form, is born.

Awakened ~ Unconditional Love, it encompasses all.

Kerry Kirwan 3/5/2018

Experiencing the Twin Flame Reunion?

I know that the twin flame journey is an immense challenge and not an easy experience to navigate, particularly if you are already in a marriage or a relationship. It ignites an inner alchemy, a fire that is all-consuming, and it was an experience that was there to destroy any remaining illusions that I may have had about finding what I was looking for outside of myself.

I see it as a great test. Was I going to be tempted by something that was external to myself and settle for less than I deserved or am destined for? I needed to be able to acknowledge that all I felt and experienced was actually occurring within myself. Even if it appeared to be coming from something or someone else externally, I had to realise that he was only a reflection of that which I needed to experience, acknowledge, integrate and live from within my own being.

Was I going to settle for something that was dependent upon an external circumstance? Or was I going to embody inner unification and function from a place that no longer identified with polarities and the sense of separation?

Twin flames are united from within whether they are in a relationship together or not; the other is not separate – they only appear to be.

I wanted to experience for myself what I experienced in the presence of my twin flame. I didn't want my experience to be dependent on another or a particular circumstance. If it arises from within and is integrated there, then it can never be taken away or longed for. I also knew that I should not become attached to what I experienced.

I know the temptation to fall in love with the reflection is enormous and extremely hard to resist. We must ask ourselves where is it that we feel what we feel and experience what we experience. It is within. We are the love we seek; we are the love that we are now experiencing; we are that which emerges from the union of the masculine and feminine; we are the divine – this is Christ consciousness.

Love's Illusion

She caught my attention because she had been there for many weeks.
I knew symbolically there must be a reason
to notice this little feathered creature.
A little bird perched in front of our spare bedroom window.
I passed her often then something made me question her behaviour.
I realised she was looking at herself; she had fallen in love with her reflection,
the one she believed was her lover.
She danced and flapped while admiring her reflection.
She was seeking love and affection.
She could not leave under any circumstance
because then she'd suffer without the romance.
A self-made jail;
Her own reflection was the veil.
A veil that needed to be lifted in order for her to
realise love doesn't exist because of the perceived other.

Kerry Kirwan

Twin flames allow each other to experience the completion of inner unification, to experience a divine level of existence. They are representative of our divine masculine and feminine counterparts. Through the unification of polarities, love emerges – an experience that can then be shared with many.

Masculine and Feminine Qualities

Masculine Energy – Yang – Left-Brain – Doing – Giving Symbol – Sunlight – Positive – Right-Side – Outer-Mind
Achiever, Aggressive, Active, Analytical, Assertive, Impatient, Hard, Dominant, Rigid, Competitive, Controlling, Confident, Forceful, Form, Independent, Individualistic, Intellectual, Strong, Logical, Self-Confident, Stable, Goal Oriented.

Feminine Energy – Yin – Right-Brain – Being – Receiving Symbol – Moon – Dark – Negative – Left-Side – Inner-Heart
Surrendered, Intuitive, Creative, Collective, Calm, Patient, Receptive, Soft, Submissive, Allowing, Fluid, Formless, Compassionate, Emotional, Expressive, Passive, Sensitive, Sensual, Affectionate, Loving, Graceful, Nurturing, Flexible, Process Oriented.

Each of us has access to all of the above qualities. Some of them are utilised and some are not, but all are important. For thousands of years, our masculine energy has dominated, repressing the feminine. Now is the time to bring them into balance. The feminine needs to rise and unite with the masculine. When they work together harmoniously, they are powerful and transformative.

Integrating and unifying from within all of the above qualities and aspects is essential to the awakening process.

The minute I heard my first love story, I started looking for you, not knowing how blind that was. Lovers don't finally meet somewhere. They are in each other all along.
—Rumi

Beyond Religion: Christ Consciousness and the Second Coming of Christ

Throughout my upbringing, I had never been introduced to religion or the like. I had no idea about spiritual beliefs, teachings or spiritual journeys, nor the purpose of spiritual teachers, masters or gurus.

From a very young age, I definitely had an unconscious aversion to religion. I wouldn't say my aversion was particularly related to God, Christ or Jesus. It was in regard to intuitively knowing that the context man had placed them in – religion – never personally resonated with me.

I believe I must have sensed the limited perspectives and perceptions others had in relationship to religion. If I heard the word God or saw images of Jesus, my unconscious conditioning would automatically place God and Jesus with religion, and I would feel myself recoil and inwardly reject it all. I can now see that it was very reflective and symbolic of me rejecting my own divinity.

Looking back now, I see that I was throwing the baby out with the bath water. I can now discern for myself that it was not that I really wanted to reject God or Christ. It was religion that I was rejecting because of the limitations I believed man had created within it, such as rules, ignorance, unconscious beliefs and false truths.

Through my own personal experiences, I came to understand that the absence of a father figure is symbolic and representative of the disconnection from the divine, God, our inner father. A workshop I conducted in 2015 confirmed my insight, and all who were participating realised the same common thread between themselves. When we become aware of the disconnection through acknowledging the sense of separation we have within, it is the calling from the inner father, God, the movement within our seed. This call is what I answered and was the voice that constantly guided me to reconcile my sense of unhappiness. However, I was totally ignorant and oblivious for many years to the fact that God/Divine was the driving force within me and the orchestrator of my awakening.

As I have shared already, symbolic images and experiences that were related to God and Jesus haven't always been predominant throughout my life and my spiritual journey. When my seeking first began in 1989, however, Jesus made his presence felt and continued to do so for many years that followed.

Not all the truths that Jesus taught are to be taken literally; his teachings are very symbolic and have far deeper meaning. Our hearts can interpret the teachings of Jesus far easier than our minds, especially once the heart centre is open as it intuitively knows. Our personal inner experiences in relationship to Jesus and the integration of his divine attributes will verify that knowing.

Each experience I had that related to Jesus was an aspect of something greater, waiting to be understood, although at the time of having them I did not realise that. That understanding only came after many years of looking back at all the experiences in their entirety. I was unconsciously waiting for them to culminate so I could realise their highest significance. Jesus and his attributes are symbolic of Christ consciousness, something we all have the ability to embody, and this was one of the processes throughout my journey that I was unknowingly going through via the integration of my masculine and feminine energies.

The story of Jesus has a well-known aspect whereby he dies and is resurrected. When we die, we know that everything will have to be relinquished in that moment. I can totally relate to this aspect because it's a symbolic aspect of the spiritual journey that I embarked upon. Although it was a slow dying process – I died while still being alive. The awakening process required me to relinquish every aspect of what I believed myself to be, including patterns of behaviour, conditioning, attachments and beliefs. It wasn't all stripped away at once; it was done little by little so the mind could cope and adjust. Once I surrendered to this process, I was resurrected in a whole new way. The second coming of Christ is within, where we can experience heaven on earth.

Before I moved to Cairns, I would see a faint vision in meditation when I asked where it was our family needed to be. I would always see a tree line across a skyline, but until we moved to Cairns I did not know what this represented. Wherever you are in Cairns, when you look into the distance, this is all you ever see – the trees upon the mountains meet the sky.

It's a point where heaven meets earth, and it was very symbolic, representing what needed to occur within me.

When many first embark on their spiritual quest, they think it's about becoming something and getting somewhere, but that couldn't be further from the truth. It's a process of removal, not one of accumulation. It's a process of annihilation, and it's painful – like having your skin ripped from your being while your insides decompose and your bones are left to dry out until they turn to dust and blow away in the wind. It's a process of purification until nothing remains.

My whole journey has been one whereby I have been stripped to the core essence of my being, and within that process there have been many other processes. One of which was reconciling all that was in conflict. Everything that was out of balance came under the symbolic aspect of either being masculine or feminine in nature. This needed to occur for Christ consciousness to be experienced as each aspect needed to be balanced and unified, which then orchestrated a divine marriage from within.

Once those duel aspects united, I ascended to a higher level of being, and my consciousness expanded into Christ consciousness – unconditional love. I witnessed the fullness of my being emerging from the emptiness.

My experience in Burma in 2002 was representative of this moment expressing itself physically, and it was the confirmation of a major pinnacle within my life in regard to the completion of all the work that had been accomplished for this to occur.

When I realised Jesus, God and the Christ energy were a predominant aspect of my journey, I became more interested in the story of Jesus and what he had come to teach. I discovered that I lived instinctively by many of the teachings of Jesus – it was already my nature, my natural state of being and how I behaved, particularly as a child – and as an adult it was still beneath the layers of conditioning.

Divine attributes are forgiveness, empathy, compassion, healing, unification and unconditional love; we can communicate telepathically with the higher levels of consciousness when our heart, third eye and crown centres have opened. The second coming of Christ is a connection with the God source – it means we return to our true nature, the divine, and we can then recognise it in others.

I happened to come across a movie called *The Last Temptation of Christ*. The title intrigued me somewhat, particularly because I had come to understand that Jesus had been making his presence felt in my life. I had come to a point where I knew that I needed to let Jesus and God become free from their association with religion.

I've always been open to the many paths available but I've never restricted myself to one particular path. There are many aspects of different paths that I have been drawn to throughout my journey, such as Sufism, which is a probably my favourite. I have also appreciated the work and teachings of many of the great teachers and masters, such as Rumi and Shams, Buddha, Osho, Yogananda, Krishna Murti, Mother Meera and Mary Magdalene, just to name a few.

I was excited to watch *The Last Temptation of Christ*. It was a very long film and because I was home alone and not distracted, I was totally absorbed in it. I was mesmerised by what was happening. Being so enthralled, I hadn't known that my energy was expanding with every passing moment. It was building and

building, intensifying with every scene of the film that I was watching and witnessing.

The more I watched, the more engrossed I became in the film. I felt like I was there as a character in the film, and it also felt like it was all transpiring within me. It built to a point that would be frighteningly realised towards the end of the movie, where Jesus had recognised that he had taken a wrong turn in life and thought that he hadn't fulfilled what he had come here to do. Right at this moment in the movie with the energy that had been building, Jesus, the movie scene and me had unknowingly fused as one. I too gasped deeply with Jesus as he made his realisation, and in that moment, I understood that this too was one of my greatest fears. I wasn't expecting this moment to transpire, and because the energy had built to such an intensity, it created an enormous thundering clap directly above our house, which was terrifyingly powerful and deafening.

I was shaken to the core. Tears were streaming down my face because of what had just happened, literally, and within the movie in relationship to Jesus. One of my greatest fears had just been exposed. The experience was so powerful that it blew out the power in the whole street.

I wandered out to the front yard, looking back towards the house and trying to assimilate what had just happened, somewhat shocked and still shaking from the experience, wondering how long it would be until the power was back on. I was also devastated that I couldn't continue to watch the movie to see the end of it until the power was returned. Later that evening, once the power was restored, I continued to watch the rest of the movie. What remained for me to view did not have as much impact as what the earlier content of it had instigated. Although I did acknowledge that without suffering many of us will never question our existence, and the cause of our suffering is because we identify with a false sense of self.

Not Christian or Jew or Muslim, not Hindu. Buddhist, Sufi, or Zen. Not any religion or cultural system. I am not from the East or the West, not out of the ocean or up from the ground, not natural or ethereal, not composed of elements at all. I do not exist, am not an entity in this world or in the next, did not descend from Adam and Eve or any origin story. My place is placeless, a trace of the traceless. Neither body nor soul.
I belong to the beloved, have seen the two worlds as one and that one call to and know, first, last, outer, inner, only that breath breathing human being.

–Rumi

10

A Forgotten Language: Symbolism, Intuition and Dreams

Using symbolism and its interpretations is something that has assisted me greatly on my life's journey. I unearthed this naturally for myself through the experiences I was having.

My dreams have been particularly revealing and are one of my favourite tools; they offer insight, intuition and confirmation and are there to assist personal growth. Dreams speak directly to me via symbolism and feelings.

Throughout this book I have shared many of my significant dreams; they were very clear in their symbolism and were relevant to my journey at the time I had them. I also relished all symbols and their meanings as I knew that it was a means for the universe, God or the divine to communicate with me.

I accepted that I was always assisted far more than I recognised at the time; there were many unspoken ways in which I was always supported in life. It was up to me to take responsibility and acknowledge the connection between everything and everyone, realising that I could work with what was being revealed.

Living life more consciously was one way to do that, and identifying the signs that the universe continually provided me through various channels assisted me significantly in life. Analysing symbols allowed me to interpret the messages that the universe was trying to give me.

These symbols came to me in everyday life, particularly via what I observed through the experiences I had within my family, the workplace, dreams, stories, art and writing. Life, in general, offered great insight if I took the time to notice the signs that were trying to get my attention.

The key is to notice the phenomena that surround us and look more deeply into the situations we experience. If I were to see an abundance of butterflies hovering closely around me in places that I wouldn't likely see them, I would question myself and ask what a butterfly means to me. What kind of life do I think a butterfly might have? How does a butterfly exist? What kind of personality do I sense a butterfly might have? How would I describe a butterfly? How is a butterfly unique? How does a butterfly come into being? How do I care for a butterfly? If I were to describe a butterfly to a person who knows nothing whatsoever about them, how would I do that?

These types of questions can be applied to anything in life, not only dreams, objects, people, places, settings and situations – particularly if there is a pattern that is repeating or something is in abundance and vying for our attention.

Once we answer these types of questions, we will be able to relate the answers to something in our life that we may have been struggling with. Our responses to the questions will give us an answer or some insight about how to best understand and cope with a situation – or it may just be a message that we need to hear at the time.

We could ask ourselves all of the above questions and even take it one step further by writing ourselves a message that contains aspects of all the answers to the questions we have analysed.

Doing this exercise would give us an overall insight that we may not have ordinarily acknowledged. We can apply questions to all things in life as everything is symbolic of something and has something deeper to reveal to us.

Intuition comes in many ways, one of which is through symbols, where we may be given information in the way of images in our mind's eye or thought forms, like imagining mountains or seeing ourselves in certain circumstances such as walking along a seaside. This too is a symbolic way of receiving messages that are not in the form of words spoken directly to us, although if recognised and analysed in the context of what we may have been concerned about, this modality will provide the answers we seek.

When my family and I relocated from Cairns to Brisbane in 2010, we lived in a few rented places in the suburbs of Brisbane. They were places that we didn't really feel comfortable in, and we felt that we were not where we were supposed to be.

I asked where we should be living, which was around the same time I commenced a yoga teacher's course that I saw advertised at a studio I went to. They also had a studio in Wynnum where the course was going to be held. I didn't really do the course to teach yoga, I only did it because I was inspired to for some reason yet unknown.

Usually when I asked where we should live, I'd get a thought image of me walking along a seaside esplanade. I used to walk

the esplanade in Cairns, and before we left, we lived very close to it. I just thought I was missing what I had.

I came to see that Wynnum was a lovely area of Brisbane; it felt more relaxed than all the other suburbs that I'd previously lived in. Unexpectedly, we were asked to vacate the home we were renting as the owners had decided they wanted to move back in.

We then decided that we would try to find something in Wynnum as it was an area close to our business. We were struggling to find something available that we liked. We persisted, and a real estate agent let us know of something that hadn't yet been put on the market to rent. It was beautiful and exactly what we wanted, although a little more expensive to rent than we would have liked, but we loved the location so paid the asked price.

Our new location happened to be two streets from the waterfront and had a lovely paved walkway we could follow for miles. As I walked along it, I understood that I was being shown where we would live all along. I just didn't realise it at the time as I'd associated it with our previous location. When I made this realisation, my heart overflowed with gratitude, and my eyes welled with tears of joy. I have always been guided in so many ways throughout my life.

It is always best to analyse symbols according to our own interpretation as everyone's perception of something is based on their personal experience and analogy, which can vary from person to person. Fire can mean warmth and comfort to one person and death and destruction to another because of a previous experience they may have had with it.

Keeping a dream journal next to my bed and recording the date before going to sleep has always been a favourite tool of mine. If I had a question that I was concerned about, I wrote that down before going to bed. Usually the important dreams were the ones I had upon waking. If I was too tired to record the whole dream, I just wrote some quick notes about it to help me recall it at a later time. I always paid particular attention to the feelings as well as the theme of the dream and the elements within it.

DREAM JOURNALING

I would like to encourage you to also keep a dream journal. Once you have written your dream out fully in your journal, it is valuable to give it a title, a title like a movie has – doing this also provides you with insight to the meaning of your dream. Having a dream buddy to work with is also beneficial; they can ask you the questions that relate to the elements in your dream and prod you to give more information where it's needed.

The major elements of a dream are its setting: people, animals, objects, feelings and plots/actions. Dreams reveal to us the way we think and feel, not what we pretend to think and feel. We can be dishonest with ourselves when we are awake but not when we are sleeping. Dreams can offer amazing insight that we may ordinarily not recognise.

Locating all the suggested elements by highlighting them, each with a different colour that relates to each element, and then symbolically interpreting them can help us to bridge meaning to our questions, or something that is relevant in our lives at the time. Interpretation happens according to our answers to the questions we or another asks about each element, and doing so will allow for an amazing depth of insight or creative inspiration, which will lead to personal discoveries and a more fulfilled richer life.

First we must look at the interpretation of the elements within the dream subjectively. We then see if we can relate personally to the questions we have answered from our dream. Most dreams are for our own personal understanding and help us to perceive where we may be blocked and not seeing things clearly. If we can't relate personally then look to see where our descriptions may relate to another or a situation that is happening in our waking life.

For example, if Aunt Mary is in our dream and we would normally describe her as shy and withdrawn, and sometimes depressed, depending on the rest of the context of the dream we may be challenged to look at our own shy, withdrawn and depressed aspects to discover what we can do about them.

If we have an animal in our dream that is wounded and we are helping it to heal, we can look at how we would describe that animal and its personality and see if we are working on healing those aspects within ourselves.

There are many different types of dreams – some are more visionary and show us the future as I have shared in previous chapters. Some dreams are there to assist us personally by what they reveal or they give us confirmation of something we have completed, which are the dreams I've shown how to work with in this chapter.

PROPHETIC OR PREDICTIVE DREAMS

This is an example of one of these dreams. When my daughter was in her last year of primary school, I had a dream about her. It was a very simple, quick and direct dream that certainly got my attention. In my dream, I was observing her from the waist up, and there was an arm that was across her waist. I was watching intently, and as I watched, I noticed that the arm began to lift. I kept watching, and as the arm rose higher and higher, it revealed an erect penis in its totality. I gasped in shock and woke myself up out of the dream.

This dream really disturbed me, particularly because of the obvious. If I'd taken the dream literally, I would have easily been misled, possibly thinking that she was being molested. I knew the dream had an important meaning that I needed to identify so I looked at it the same way I look at all dreams – symbolically. I asked myself what this dream was trying to tell me. I realised that there was something connected to my daughter that I was not seeing clearly, something that was hidden, and it was something from the waist up. I understood the penis was there to get my attention, so there was something about my daughter that needed attention, something that I was not seeing clearly. The clarity I'd come to then made me ask, 'Okay, what am I not seeing clearly that is connected to my daughter?'

Prior to the dream, I had noticed that one of my daughters' breasts looked larger than her other one; it appeared to be growing at a different rate to the other. After noticing, I didn't think too much about it, although thought I'd just keep an eye on her.

Within the week of the dream, I happened to have the television on in the afternoon and there was a documentary about scoliosis being aired. I was drawn to watch it, so I sat down to watch it as I found it interesting. Later that afternoon, I was on the back patio and my daughter came home from school and walked to the freezer to get an icy pole, which was in the laundry.

As she walked to the laundry, I just happened to glance up and noticed her back. I then had a massive ah ha moment. I saw

that the problem was with her back; it appeared thicker on one side, more than it did on the other. It was not her breast that was the problem; it was her back that was twisting and causing her breast to appear more protruded on one side than it did the other. I immediately booked her in to be seen by a doctor and her diagnosis was scoliosis.

She had a 30-degree curvature in her upper back and a 20-degree in her lower back. We were then recommended to specialists that organised a brace for her to wear 24 hours a day for two years, which ended up being three. Her back required assistance to stop it from becoming worse, and the only time she could remove the brace was to have a shower. So, as you can recognise clearly from this dream, we are assisted to acknowledge what we need to realise. This is not always literally; it is often in ways that we may bypass if we are not living consciously and taking notice.

I had seen that there was something not right with my daughter although I hadn't seen clearly what the problem was. So, I was given the dream and the dream was also supported by a television program. Because I questioned and analysed my dream, it all came together perfectly, and my daughter's issue was addressed and action was taken far more quickly than it possibly would have been if it were left unattended to.

Some dreams are self-explanatory and do not need clarification, but the following dreams need more in-depth interpreting.

TEETH DREAMS

Many times, I have had a dream whereby I have tugged on a tooth or touched it and the rest came tumbling out after it. I'd spit profusely tooth after tooth into my hand. It was a distressing dream because I'd try to put my teeth back where they came from, but it was not ever possible to do so, nor could a dentist do it.

For me, the meaning of this dream relates to once something has been transformed or changed dramatically, it can never return to the way it had been prior.

Whenever I was about to go through major shifts and changes, particularly within myself, it was likely that I would have a teeth dream of this nature.

CLEARING AND PURIFYING DREAMS
Many times when I was clearing deeply embedded patterns or conditioning, I'd have dreams whereby I might pick at something on my leg and see something there and I'd then begin to pull at it. I would end up pulling and pulling; I'd feel repulsed, and it would be like a worm or a piece of string that I'd keep winding up like a ball of wool. I'd be pulling out more and more; it would just keep coming like there was no end to it. I'd be absolutely astounded at how much was continuing to come and was wondering if there would ever be an end to what was being removed. This type of dream indicates that the removal of deeply embedded personal or collective identification with a particular pattern or conditioning has taken place.

Questions you can ask in relationship to the elements in your dream:

FEELINGS
What was the feeling you had upon waking from the dream?
What were the feelings you were most aware of in the dream?
Have you felt this way in your past or in current life?
When or where was the first time you felt this way?

SETTINGS
Describe the setting in the dream.
What is this place like in your dream?
How does it feel to be in this setting?
Does this setting remind you of anything in your waking life?
What type of people do you find in this setting?
Is what's happing in your dream typical of this setting? If not, how is it different?

PEOPLE AND ANIMALS = A
Who is A?
Tell me about A.
What kind of person or animal is A?
How do you feel about A?
What is A doing in your dream?
What kind of person/animal do you imagine A might be?
What kind of personality do you think A might have?
How do you feel about A being in your dream?
Is there anyone in your waking life that reminds you of A in your dream?

OBJECTS = B
What is a B?
What is a B used for?
What types of people have or use a B?
How does a B work?
Do you like B? Why or why not?

ACTION/PLOT
Describe major actions. Do they remind you of anything or situations in waking life? If so, how so?
How would you describe the plot or main action happening in the dream?
Does it remind you of any situations in waking life?
Is this action or plot typical in life? If not, how is it different?
Do the actions in the dream evoke feelings?

The heart has its own language. The heart knows a hundred thousand ways to speak.

There is another language beyond language, another place beyond heaven and hell. Precious gems come from another mine, the heart draws light from another source.
                                                            –Rumi

11:11
Its Purpose and Meaning

I have seen the number sequence 11.11 since my childhood. I began to notice it when digital clocks became popular in the 1970s. I only ever noticed 11:11 periodically on my digital clock; I hadn't noticed it anywhere else at that stage and had no idea why I was noticing it. I was not aware that it would be connected to the journey that I was to embark upon as an adult, nor did I know at the time how it would become related. The understanding of 11:11 unfolded as my inner journey did.

In my late teens, I remember 11:11 being discussed briefly by my family members. I was surprised when I realised that I was not the only one who was noticing it. But we didn't understand that it had any relevance, and still didn't after we discussed it. Although, this only made me more curious about it because I thought I was the only one that was seeing it and wondered why.

I was intrigued and wanted to discover the purpose of the 11:11 phenomena. I have been pursuing its meaning and purpose simultaneously while discovering my own reason for

being and purpose. My first ever psychic reading in 1990 happened to be at 11 a.m. on the 11th. I thought to myself at the time, *What is this 11:11 about?* It wasn't long after the reading, when I was attending one of the channelled sessions, that a friend just randomly held up a book and said, 'I think you would be interested in this.' I was blown away by the cover; it had a massive 11:11 in the middle of it. I bought the book by Solara and started to read it, hoping for some answers and clarity. Unfortunately, a lot of what I read in the book didn't make sense to me. The words and the explanations were beyond my intellectual capacity in regard to spiritual matters and my comprehension of them. It was frustrating as I had no mentor at the time to tell me that it was okay and that this would all make sense one day.

In the coming years, I noticed 11:11 everywhere; it was usually the time I turned my light out for the evening. I saw it on car number plates, on my phone, hotel room numbers and so many other places.

My initials are KK, and K is the 11th letter of the alphabet. My soul urge number in numerology is 11, both my children's birthdates add to 11 and the times they were born add to 11. I have unintentionally been given appointments that end up being on the 11th at 11 a.m., and the person I had the twin flame experience with has KK for his initials. I was invited to a friend's apartment overseas, and her address was on the 11th floor and the apartment number was 11. These were just a few of so many incidents where 11:11 revealed itself to me.

The Symbology of 11 – New York City 911 incident.
11:11 was very predominant in the Twin Towers incident in New York, and the date it happened was 11th of the 9th –

911/11. The towers also looked like a giant number 11. New York is the 11th State of America. The first plane to crash was flight 11, and it was carrying 92/11 passengers. The second flight had 65/11 passengers, and the total number of passengers killed on all the aircrafts was 254/11. September 11 is the 254th/11 day in the calendar year.

I always look at everything symbolically, so I see this incident as an external reflection that is representative of the destruction/collapse of duality and the resurrection of unity within humanity, which is what 11:11 represents.

The two towers were replaced by one single beam of light, which is also symbolic of unity. I know this was a truly devastating incident for many who observed and experienced it. I'm not in any way trivialising or condoning what happened. I just endeavour to look beyond appearances to find greater significance and meaning within these experiences.

This incident for me was the confirmation that the work many had been doing in regard to transitioning from a dualistic nature to one of unification had been established. Many of us had been through a process whereby we were torn down and resurrected in a new way, and destruction allows for change and resurrection.

There are many theories regarding the meaning and the purpose of 11:11. I will give my theory and share the realisations that I have discovered from my personal experience of it. I have discovered that my personal seeking to know who I am and the seeing of 11:11 were always part of the planned unfolding of my journey to awaken.

I had only ever seen these two aspects separately, and I did not relate them to each other at all for a long period of time. It took many years to see just how entwined those two aspects

were, and that they were not separate – they only appeared to be. I had no idea that my spiritual seeking and 11:11 were related to the degree that they were.

At the beginning of my seeking, nothing much made sense. I didn't have any idea where it was all leading, and my mind was unable to conceptualise what was happening. It didn't have the capacity to see or know the bigger picture at that time. I just had to trust the process that I was going through.

A symbolic analogy: I was identified with a part that hadn't yet experienced and realised its totality. Similar to a drop returning to an ocean, it had to be willing to expand beyond what it thought it was, to understand that it was something far greater. The perceived drop had to expand and lose its sense of a small self to reach its depth and width, thus acknowledging and experiencing its vastness.

This same analogy relates to the understanding of the process I went through in relationship to my journey and how everything was an aspect of that process. I couldn't see or understand the process until it had all played out and had been fully experienced and accepted. Only then could I look back upon my journey in its totality to recognise and see how all the aspects of my process were interrelated and part of the whole experience.

Eleven is a master number; it represents illumination and spiritual enlightenment. 11:11 is related to awakening and is a code programmed to activate within humanity's DNA; it is a divine reminder, a time to remember who we are.

11:11 is symbolic of inner unification, the result of all conflicts being balanced from within. It represents the unity of the masculine and feminine and also relates to the twin flame 11:11 journey. It is symbolic of a divine marriage that allows us to experience the love that we are, and beyond. It is representative of the journey that one embarks upon to attain Christ consciousness and God realisation.

My personal journey allowed me to accept that 11:11 is a code that has been pre-encoded into humanity's DNA. It is a reminder, a trigger, something that makes us question why. Questioning why we are seeing 11:11 and questioning who we are will then allow life to reveal the answer to us.

We are not only a separate individualised aspect; we are something so much greater that is yet to be realised. In order to understand and experience what that is, we have to be willing to relinquish our limited self into what that is – the vastness that contains everything.

I will reiterate what my teacher said to me, 'The journey is not for the faint of heart.' I discovered that we have to be willing to surrender all that we believe ourselves to be and all that we have been conditioned by. We must be willing to take responsibility and do the work that's required, renouncing all that has been identified with inwardly and externally.

11:11 is a symbolic representation of the spiritual path that one takes to reveal the truth. 11:11 is there to wake us up, and it is connected to the Christ energy, which Jesus is symbolic of, and it is representative of the process we go through to integrate Christ consciousness. 11:11 represents moving beyond all that is dualistic in nature to a place of wholeness and unification. This process opens the inner doorway to love and is the happiness that we all seek in life, which is realised from within.

I believe those who do notice 11:11 are the ones who are ready to awaken and realise who they are beyond their individualisation, their ego self. The second coming of Christ is not

through one individual person being born to this word. It will occur through the many that are already here.

If you have read this far then you too are one of the seeds that are ready to germinate, grow and bloom. Life will be your fertiliser, and the story you live will burn away all that is in the way of your process to self-realisation. Christ consciousness will reside in the centre of your being. The unification of the masculine and feminine is a divine marriage that will bloom into the awareness that we are all an expression of the same essence: Love.

I am a hole in a flute that the Christ's breath moves through. Listen to this music, I am the concert from the mouth of every creature, singing with the myriad chorus. I am a hole in a flute that the Christ's breath moves through, listen to this music.

–Hafiz

Important Realisations

FEAR

What we identify with is that which limits us as it's a self-made prison. Fear particularly is something that we have been unconsciously conditioned by and could now be identifying with. It is extremely beneficial to those in power if this is the case.

Those in positions of power know how to control us if we function from this state of being, and don't for a minute think that they won't use that to their advantage. This is just one reason we should know who we are.

Fear is the barrier to love; love has no opposite. Become conscious of fear and its predominance in the world, notice how many businesses use fear in their advertising, how the media uses fear, how governments use fear. Become aware of where it may be used to manipulate situations and where we may be manipulated by it at the hands of others. When we recognise fear and choose to respond and act from a place of love, in place of fear, life will dramatically change for us, which is another reason it's important to know and experience who we are and realise what we're not.

ADDICTION

Substance abuse and addiction is another way that we are easily controlled. When we are influenced by such things, we are not present in our own power – we are giving it away. Substance abuse opens us up to be taken advantage of as we do not make decisions that have our best interests at heart – how can we? We are not present and functioning optimally; our consciousness is in an altered state that can't be fully present. Again, it is a limitation and keeps us small and controlled.

This is another state that those in power like us to be in because we then give our power to them to take advantage of. We must take back our power and become responsible for our state of being. We need to look at why we feel the need to check out of life. What or who are we trying to escape? It will be surprise when we realise the answer; the answer is why those in power like to keep us where we are, limited and small.

Empowered people make empowered choices and live empowered lives. Who we are and our connection with everything is always present no matter our circumstances, but an induced altered state stops us from functioning from that aspect. We must ask ourselves where the disconnection is. What have we disconnected from? Someone can point the way although we hold the key to open that door in order to experience it.

FEELINGS

It is always important to pay attention to what we feel. What we feel is a feminine aspect, but because the feminine has been somewhat suppressed, this is one of the attributes that is not being fully utilised. Feeling is something that allows knowing or gives us greater awareness. It is somewhat intuitive. We have been conditioned to believe that our feelings are not valid, but to have this belief is limiting – to not allow ourselves to feel is even more limiting.

Often feeling has been suppressed because we may fear pain, and sometimes we shut feelings off because we do not want to take responsibility for the knowing that's evoked from these feelings. We believe that it is better to remain ignorant. Making a conscious effort to get in touch with what we feel will offer surprising information and will help us live a more authentic life.

GRIEF
Grief is something we usually associate with losing someone close to us, such as the death or loss of another. I have come to accept that the loss of our divine self creates grief and pain that is far, far greater than any other form of grief as we have lost ourselves. I have not ever seen this type of grief discussed at all, and many do not even know it exists. It is like a deep sadness that can't be escaped; its reason for being can only be understood when we have the courage to face it and do something about it.

Never be afraid to ask why we feel the way we do. We need to remain open and allow the answers to come to us. Grief lingers within us like a dark heaviness deep inside; we can sense it there but we don't know its reason for being because we haven't realised our disconnection from our true self – the Divine-God. I'm sure many feel it but mistake it for depression, masking it with medication or substance abuse. Reconnecting with the divine within ourselves will lift the sadness and heal the grief we suffer.

AWAKENING - SPIRITUALITY - SELF-RELISATION

We must be mindful not to relinquish one garment and put on another – being spiritual these days has become fashionable. So many talk the language but do not walk their talk. Spirituality has become big business; we can begin a spiritual journey and get distracted along the way, caught up in the temptations to be something – a psychic, a medium, a healer, a counsellor, a light worker. We want to help people, fix people, do good.

Spirituality's true purpose and meaning has become somewhat diluted. We must be mindful to not be too distracted by all that's purple and sparkling. We should not become attached to what doesn't serve our highest purpose. We can work in this way, although don't become too attached to it or identified with it. Experiences are just that – experiences. Allow them to pass as we are not our experiences – they only allow for awareness.

We need to keep doing the work for ourselves first and foremost as we can only change ourselves. Be dedicated and devoted to the spiritual path of awakening. To fulfil life's greatest purpose we must never allow ourselves to be distracted from experiencing who we are. Realise that everything is perfect as it is, and the only place we can make lasting change is within ourselves. We need to become our own masterpiece; we are not here to save the world, nobody needs fixing and we will eventually come to the realisation that there is no other. Nothing can be added to or subtracted from. Nothing comes or goes – love is all there is – emptiness and fullness.

We were green: we ripened and grew golden.
The sea terrified us: we learned how to drown.

Squat and earthbound, we unfolded huge wings.

We started to sober: are love's startled drunkards.

You hide me in your cloak of nothingness. Reflect my ghost in your glass of being, I am nothing, yet appear: transparent dream where your eternity briefly trembles.

–Rumi

A MASTER OR TEACHER

We can observe from my journey of awakening that our journeys are not linear. There are many processes happening on many levels, simultaneously, each unfolding and relating to the other. Only when everything has culminated will clarity and understanding arise. To have someone who has walked the path before us is extremely beneficial. A teacher or a master knows the pitfalls along the way so can hold the space and reflect to us what needs to be acknowledged and integrated from within.

A teacher or a master has no expectation, motive or agenda – they are the one who is there to assist us through our transition by being who they are, which helps us to establish that same level of awareness within us. The presence of a teacher or master will speed up our process. They are a God-given gift to those who are dedicated and devoted to the path of self-realisation. They are there for those of us who will not be satisfied until we have discovered the answer to the questions: Who Am I and why am I here?

STORY & REFLECTION

I came to accept that my story is just that – a story. One that is filled with what appears to be many others, each character playing an important role to help me to realise who I am.

We all have our own unique story and will continue to be a part of one after we have discovered the purpose of our stories.

Our stories have been choreographed by the divine so we can realise our true selves. The role and characters that others play in our stories are just like actors who fulfil their role in a movie to bring about a desired conclusion. The characters will expose everything about us that veils that truth. Others, the characters in our story, will do that by reflecting to us what we most need to acknowledge so we can move beyond any limitations that we may have become attached to. Those limitations will usually be greatly magnified so we can perceive them, and those who play that role will generally push our buttons – whatever we resist will persist.

It is important not to get caught in the conflict that may arise as conflict isn't with the other. It's within us and is representative of whatever the perception of the other is evoking in us. It's important to understand what it is that the other is revealing to us about ourselves. We will need to acknowledge it by taking responsibility for it and be willing to change something from within that relates to the pattern or conditioning that's being exposed so the that we can be freed from it.

I once watched a documentary whereby a large mirror was placed into a chimpanzee's enclosure at a zoo. There were many chimps in the enclosure and most were inquisitive, inspecting the mirror and their reflection. But they realised after a period of time that they were observing themselves. They moved away and found a place to relax in another area of their compound.

One particular chimpanzee was obsessed with his reflection; he became extremely agitated and angry. He could not see that it was his reflection. All he could see was an angry, agitated other that he felt he needed to dominate and control; therefore, he became trapped in a battle with himself for hours. He could not recognise that what he seen and what was reflected was one and the same. Don't fall into the same trap. So many become caught in their own reflection, which isn't real, and never realise the truth for lifetime after lifetime.

JUDGEMENT & RESISTANCE
Be mindful of judgements as they enforce separation. Instead of judging, acknowledge and be with whatever is happening without resistance. Dual aspects are not separate; they are one end of the spectrum opposed to the other, with varying degrees in between. Pleasure and pain, happy and sad, peaceful and angry, hot and cold – one aspect cannot be experienced without the other. Judging one as more preferred than the other creates a sense of separation between the two. A coin is comprised of two sides, heads and tails, and they can't be separated as both are required for the coin to exist in its totality.

In order for us to exist and to be whole and complete both aspects, masculine and feminine, are equally important. Where separation between the two has been made, work will be required to balance and unite them. When we judge another, we are actually judging ourselves. What we resist persists, and resistance causes pain and suffering. Try to be with whatever is happening. When we pull away from something, understand we are trying to pull away from ourselves and that's impossible to do. We can't escape ourselves; eventually, we have to recognise what we're not and realise who we are, experience it and accept it.

MIND & PURIFICATION
Emptying the mind of its content and accepting that the mind is not the master can be a challenging task to achieve. The

mind's function is a tool that can be used throughout life, but in most people's lives, it's the one in control – it has become the master. The ego mind is limited; it's an aspect that has been constructed by every experience we have unconsciously identified with. The mind does not give up without a fight because it wants to remain the master. It will try to sabotage our efforts to break free from it. It will test our resolve in the hope that we will give up and meet its demands.

What we remain unconscious about is like hosting a parasite. If a parasite remains in its host and is undetected, it will eventually take over its host and can then affect every action made and influence every experience to get its needs met. It will remain the one in control. Identifying with the mind and its content is exactly like this.

We cannot remain asleep and allow unconscious behaviours to navigate our lives by that which influences it. We must become conscious of who we are; we are not our mind's content or its thoughts. If we were infested with a parasite, it would be beneficial to cleanse ourselves to be free of it. We would clean out the space that it resides in so we are not influenced by it any longer. We have to take responsibility for our condition as it is far healthier to live our lives consciously and clean out what no longer serves us.

It is also beneficial to cleanse and purify our physical bodies, our temples. Eating cleanly assists all aspects of our being at every level. We need to be mindful of how some substances affect our bodies and our wellbeing. Feeling our best can sometimes be as simple as providing ourselves with certain vitamins and minerals that are lacking. Exercise is also great; it helps our energy flow rather than stagnate.

MEDITATION

Meditation is the perfect way to withdraw ourselves from the world, from all the noise and distractions. Our souls need this time to recalibrate. Meditation gives us the space we need to be with ourselves. It's a time to connect more deeply with who we are when all the noise and distractions aren't there. We must learn to love our own company – it's the perfect time to empty out all that has accumulated. It centres our being by aligning what is out of balance, it clears our thoughts and brings a sense of calm by bringing us closer to the still centre within our being. It allows us to have experiences that we wouldn't ordinarily have.

One of my meditations was truly amazing. There were times throughout my journey when I withdrew from the world and spent a lot of time at home alone without distractions. I would meditate when inspired to; I loved being in my own company and would sit for hours in the silence. This particular day, it was overcast and raining – the perfect day to hear the rain tinkering on the tin roof and to be watching and hearing the wind blow wildly.

One of the delights about living in the rainforest was the tree frogs; they always loved the rain and celebrated its arrival by croaking continuously back and forward to each other. During my meditation, I must have gone very deep and became conscious of how deep I was. I had no sense of my physical body – it didn't exist. I had no boundary; I was pure awareness and had become one with the elements. I was the wind and the rain, and that which controlled its intensity. I could feel its power; it was physically surging through my being. I could feel when the rain became heavier or lighter; it was like I was able to choose its intensity, and at the same time I had an awareness

of its intensity. All of it was happening within, there was no me, and at the same time I was conscious of everything. It felt like a powerful vastness that I contained and yet not.

ONENESS-DIVINE-GOD

I had no idea what Oneness/Divine meant when my journey began. I have come to understand that we can know what it means or we can experience what it means. At least if we know what it means, we can begin to understand things from that perspective and then work towards the experience. Oneness is representative of a point whereby everything is the same – nothing is separate from anything else at its core essence. Learning to see everything in this way is extremely beneficial. Particularly on our journey of awakening, knowing this allows us to take responsibility. We realise that everyone and everything is who we are, and who we are is Divine-God-One.

With this information, we can work with a new awareness, one that is based on unification with the experiences that we encounter. Many have been conditioned to see and function from a place of duality, where everything is judged as separate to everything else. It's just a change of perspective that is required. Many once thought the world was flat then a few brave adventurers explored the waters and understood it was round. They then shared their knowledge so that those who hadn't yet discovered that for themselves could change their perspective.

A change of perspective can assist us to move beyond fear so that many new realisations can arise and expansion can happen. Try to imagine that we are in everything, everything is us, and what we do to another we are actually doing to ourselves. If we see something other than the divine essence within another, it's a reflection of something that we are in denial about within us. When we point our finger at another, the other three fingers point back at us.

To become spiritual, you must die to self, and come alive in the Lord. Only then will the mysteries of God fall from your lips. To die to the self through self-discipline causes suffering but brings you everlasting life.

–Rumi

12

Conclusion

While writing this book, I could see that all the perceived limitations I worked through related to three deeply imbedded fears: fear of being seen, fear of love and fear of speaking the truth. These fears are all interrelated and are one and the same, like facets of a diamond:

- ❖ The fear of being seen and being naked was reflected constantly by the issues I was challenged with, which related to and were represented by the masculine and feminine imbalance from within. At a deeper level when we are truly naked, we are revealing who we truly are. We are not hiding anything as it's there fully exposed for all to see. It's a pure state of being where we know who we are and we reveal it to others.

  Balancing the masculine and feminine is what orchestrated my acceptance to be seen, to be naked, to be exposed, to be who I truly am and to not be afraid to let others see that. The issues I dealt with were far more

deeply rooted than I had ever perceived they were. They related to what I have just revealed, and those fears were constantly reflected back to me via the experiences that I had in life. All the layers needed to be reconciled; I had to move beyond all fear in order to accept and experience who I was: the divine.

- ❖ The fear of love is about realising love and its source, being it and having it reflected back. It is closely related to the fear of being seen, which can be symbolised by a rose in bloom. Love is its fragrance; one can't exist without the other. To be a rose and share our fragrance is symbolic of the divine in all its splendour.

- ❖ The fear of speaking our truth comes into play so that our knowledge of the other two aspects – the divine and love – can be spoken about and shared with many. This sharing helps others to recognise it for themselves. Unblocking my throat to create a clear pathway for my voice was an important challenge to overcome. This now allows me to speak and share the truth that I have discovered and experienced, speaking and sharing in a humble manner without the fear of being persecuted for doing so.

These three aspects are related to Christ consciousness. Jesus symbolically represented all of the above and lived it, as do others. We do not have to be religious to come to this understanding; we only have to question who we are and why we are here. We must then have the courage to do whatever it takes to experience the answers to these questions. We must be prepared to die while still alive, which is why the journey is not for the faint of heart.

The cover of my book has all the symbolism that relates to my journey, and it is the journey that you will be invited to embark upon when the time is right. 11:11 is representative of that time, the red rose represents Christ consciousness, and its fragrance is love that ascends from the balance of polarities, masculine and feminine. The fire represents purification. The black background is the emptiness from which everything is made possible – the place where all is witnessed.

There was once a king, who one day, entering his royal court, observed one person, whom among all those present, was not bowing down before him. Unnerved by the impudent act of this stranger in the hall, the king called out: "How dare you not bow down before me. Only God does not bow down before me, and there is nothing greater than God. Who then are you?" That tattered stranger answered with a smile,

'I am that nothing'.

Llewellyn Vaughn Lee
The Call and the Echo

ABOUT THE AUTHOR

Kerry is God-realised, married, a mother of two and a grandmother of three. She is certified in yoga and meditation and is now an author who is passionate about writing. Kerry has had numerous businesses throughout her life, the first being a fairy shop in Far North Queensland. She has also owned natural therapy businesses, conducted workshops and currently has a business with her husband in the hospitality industry. Kerry now lives in Brisbane, Australia. She loves to travel and participates in and facilitates workshops and retreats in Australia and overseas.

BLOOM & BURN

A sun is one that shines light and offers warmth because that's what it does without an agenda or expectation.

Kerry is dedicated to serving the divine and is open to supporting many on their spiritual journey of awakening. She is dedicated to those who desire to realise who they are, to 'Bloom & Burn' beyond all that is limiting. It is Kerry's belief that awakening and realising who we are can be experienced and integrated gradually while doing what we love doing best.

Everything except love is devoured by love.
—Rumi

Enjoyed the book? Kerry welcomes reviews and recommendations.

You can contact Kerry at:
kerrykirwan11.11@gmail.com

You can follow Kerry at:
kerrykirwan.com/com.au
and
https://www.facebook.com/KerryKirwan11.11/

www.ingramcontent.com/pod-product-compliance
Lightning Source LLC
Chambersburg PA
CBHW031421290426
44110CB00011B/474